COLLOQUIAL
ARABIC
(LEVANTINE)

THE COLLOQUIAL SERIES

*Accompanying cassette available

COLLOQUIAL
ARABIC
(LEVANTINE)

Leslie J. McLoughlin

Routledge

London and New York

First published in 1982
by Routledge & Kegan Paul Plc
Reprinted in 1983, 1989 and 1993
by Routledge
11 New Fetter Lane, London EC4P 4EE
29 West 35th Street, New York, NY 10001
© Leslie J. McLoughlin 1982
Printed in Great Britain
by Cox & Wyman Ltd., Reading

British Library Cataloguing in Publication Data

McLoughlin, Leslie J.

Colloquial Arabic (Levantine).
1. Arabic language – Spoken Arabic
2. Arabic language – Grammar
I. Title
492'.783421   PJ6307   80-42071

ISBN 0-415-05107-X

ISBN 0-415-01854-4 (cassette)

ISBN 0-415-00073-4 (book and cassette course)

CONTENTS

PART TWO APPENDICES

ABBREVIATIONS

adj.	Adjective
BRP	British Received Pronunciation
c.	Common (of gender)
CA	Classical Arabic
coll. A.	Colloquial Arabic
f.	Feminine
lit.	Literally
m.	Masculine
n.	Noun
pl.	Plural
prep.	Preposition
pron.	Pronoun
sing.	Singular
vb	Verb
v.n.	Verbal noun

INTRODUCTION

Arabic is the language of daily communication for between 150 and 200 million people, and the language of worship for many hundreds more millions of Muslims. It is the original language of the Koran, which in Muslim belief is incomparably excellent, since it is the direct word of God (*kalaam allaah*). Arabic is the language of prayer for all Muslims, and the language of the muezzin who summons the faithful to prayer the world over five times daily. It is now an official working language in the UN and many international agencies. Its script is used in many other languages – Persian, Ottoman Turkish and Urdu among them – and since the Koran is possibly the world's best selling book the Arabic script may well be the second most used script after Latin. The Arabic written language is almost completely uniform throughout the Arab world. Moreover the language of radio and television is uniform to the same extent, since it is simply the written word of modern Arabic being read aloud.

There is a direct line of descent from classical Arabic, the language of the Koran, to modern Arabic; so that across 1,400 years (in the Islamic calendar) the script is recognizably the same, the grammar has changed remarkably little (by comparison with, for example, German or English) and even the vocabulary has shown an astonishing integrity and consistency. It is the Koran which has preserved the essence of written Arabic, and it is also the elevated status accorded to the original language of Islam which has prevented the Arabic dialects from becoming as far apart from each other as the dialects of Latin. Whereas Italian and French are not now mutually comprehensible, the speakers of dialects of Arabic over an enormous area can understand each other. Peasants from Muscat and Morocco respectively would certainly have problems with each other's dialects, but even peasants and certainly

1

educated people throughout the Peninsula, the Levant, Iraq, Egypt, the Sudan and some parts of N. Africa can make themselves understood to each other without necessarily resorting to classical Arabic.

Within the Levant (historical Syria, Jordan and Lebanon) there is, if not linguistic homogeneity, at least clearly visible evidence of close similarity between the many dialects. The differences are what one would expect. A Sidon (Lebanon) fisherman will use different metaphors from those of a Syrian from the Jebel Druze; because of close community ties over long historical periods villages tend to preserve distinctive features of vocabulary and phonology.*

This introductory manual aims to present those features of the language which would be acceptable throughout the Levant area. The speech presented is not, on the one hand, the dialect of any particular village or area; nor is it, on the other, a debased classical form spoken by no one in particular. The aim is to present a natural form of speech, which is acceptable and at the same time idiomatic and correct.

An Arabic proverb says 'A new language is a new man' and, among other things, this means that a non-Arab approaching Arabic has to be ready to understand (if not necessarily to imitate) different attitudes and perspectives. Westerners are not in everyday speech given, as Arabs are, to quoting poetry, ancient proverbs and extracts from holy books. Nor are they wont to exchange fulsome greetings. This is to say nothing of the different attitudes to physical contact and proximity, as well as to relations between the sexes. It is, however, essential to understand not only the grammar and vocabulary of the Arabic of this area but also the underlying attitudes and assumptions.

Perhaps the greatest difference between the Levantine approach to language and that of westerners is that Levantines, like most Arabs, take pleasure in using language for its own sake.** The *sahra*

---

*This is after all the area which gave the world the concept of a shibboleth, and this same feature (*s/sh*) still distinguishes Levant dialects from each other (*sajara/shajara*; tree).

**But in a way totally different from other Arabic speakers: five minutes on the streets of Cairo reveal attitudes to life and language totally different from those of Syria.

(or evening entertainment) may well take the form of talk alone, but talk of a kind forgotten in the west except in isolated communities such as Irish villages or Swiss mountain communities – talk not merely comical, tragical, historical/pastoral, etc. but talk ranging over poetry, story-telling, anecdotes, jokes, word-games, singing and acting. It is no accident that Arabic has a verb which means 'to chat to someone in the evening' and that a common name is Samir (f. Samira) meaning 'one with whom one chats in the evening'. The moral for the non-Arab is that if one can adjust to these different attitudes to language, and understand what is going on, one can discover whole layers of Arab life which must remain unsuspected to those who know no Arabic or who, knowing some, remain attached to (for example) the belief that only classical Arabic is a fit object of study. The present writer takes the view that a real understanding and appreciation of colloquial Arabic can only expand a student's knowledge of classical Arabic. A student who understood all the allusions to poetry, proverbs and religion to be heard on a day's march in the Levant would be far beyond doctoral standards in terms of university study.*

This manual attempts to give some insight into aspects of colloquial Arabic other than syntax and vocabulary: in addition to twelve lessons on these subjects there are lessons on idioms, greetings, ritual language, terms of address and reference, proverbs, even on abuse. A multi-media approach would be necessary to do justice to a communicative approach to colloquial Arabic** (perhaps to any language) but the present volume, it is hoped, will, by presenting information in separate 'packages' on the printed pages, prepare the student's approach to mastering this most fascinating language.

*Lebanese Arabic in particular is much maligned by some orientalists. In fact a study of its vocabulary reveals a very high percentage of classical vocables.
**This manual has, perforce, to omit an essential element in everyday Levantine communication, namely hand gestures. An illustrated dictionary of the meanings of some hundreds of gestures could be (indeed, once was) compiled. These differ from Mediterranean hand gestures (with which they show some features) in that they not only reinforce meaning but can also be used to hold meaningful conversations across a distance.

THE STRUCTURE OF ARABIC

The following are brief notes on **how Arabic works**, taking ten broad features common to both written and spoken Arabic.

1 Arabic is a Semitic language (unlike Turkish and Persian), hence the similarity to Arabic of Hebrew phrases from the Bible, e.g. Matt. 27:46: 'Jesus cried with a loud voice, saying, *Eli, Eli, lamma sabachthani?* that is to say, My God, my God, why hast thou forsaken me?'

2 Semitic languages are distinguished by the **triliteral root** system. The consonants *k–t–b* imply something to do with *writing*. The addition of prefixes, infixes and suffixes generates words connected with writing.

3 The **root and pattern** system in Arabic is highly developed and, being on the whole consistent and predictable, can be used by a foreign student to guess meanings of new words and increase vocabulary. Thus, from *k–t–b*:

	Pattern	*Word*	*Remarks*
1	ma/--a-	maktab	Office, study, bureau, desk
			Pattern always means 'place of . . .'
2	-aa-i-	kaatib	Clerk, writer, author
			Pattern always means the active
			participle or doer of the action
3	ma--oo-	maktoob	Letter
			Pattern always means the passive participle
4	-aa-a-	kaatab	To correspond with someone
			Form III derived verb, usually means
			to do the action *to* someone
5	mu-aa-i-	mukaatib	Correspondent
			Active participle of (4) above

4 **Predictability** Arabic has almost complete predictability in its patterns (cf. English: light/lit; fight/fought; sight/sighted). Past-tense verbs conjugate with suffixes, for example, which are invariable for all verbs.

5 **Consistency in spelling**
(a) Words can be spelled correctly once the sound is known correctly. Not for Arabic the complexities of English: seen/scene; bean/been etc.

(b) The name of the consonant gives the consonant's
pronunciation. *Haa'* is the name of the sound registered
by *H* (cf. English: aitch = h).

6 Economy

(a) Arabic has only two tenses, past and non-past.
(b) Arabic has basically only three short vowels (*a*, *i* and *u*), three
long (*aa*, *ee* and *oo*) and two diphthongs (*ay* and *aw*).
(c) In classical Arabic the short vowels do heavy morphological
duty for verb endings, case endings and pronoun distinction, in
ways which are clearly related, for example a final /*i*/ or /*ee*/
means *you*, feminine singular, in both verbs and pronouns.
(d) In colloquial Arabic the same applies, but even more so:
colloquial has almost no case endings, and verb suffixes are far
fewer than in classical.

7 Simplicity Particularly in colloquial Arabic, sentence structure
is very simple: for example, equational sentences have no *is/are*.
Furthermore, Levantine Arabic like all Arabic dialects is much
given to expressing a great deal in highly truncated sentences and
phrases and even single words. (Cf. Egyptian multi-purpose use of
the word for yes!)

8 Stress patterns The place of the stress – or prominence – in a
word is almost completely determined by fixed rules. In broad terms
the stress falls on the first syllable *except* when the word has a long
syllable. Then the stress falls on the nearest long syllable to the end
of the word.*

9 Formality Colloquial Arabic has many ritual or formal phrases
in greeting, salutation etc. (Beware of thinking, however, that the
language is cabalistic!)

10 Intonation Particular attention should be paid by students to
native speakers' intonation: a wrong intonation is one of the clearest
markers of a foreign accent.

TRANSCRIPTION AND PRONUNCIATION

Systems of transliteration seem to vary only in degrees of repulsive-
ness. No one system is satisfactory to all, and the general reader is

---

*A long syllable is one with a long vowel or diphthong *or* a short vowel
followed by two consonants.

often deterred by an excessively scrupulous attempt to render phonetic differences.

The system employed in this book uses only the symbols found on an ordinary typewriter. In the writer's experience most of the apparent difficulties of using transliteration disappear when use is made of a recording of the text (see *How to use the book*).

Introduction to Arabic pronunciation

1 **Consonants and vowels** The table below aims to guide the beginner with a mixture of technical terms and layman's language. The recordings should also be used freely.

2 **Stress** Arabic stress rules are quite different from English, and failure to observe this is one of the principal features of a foreign accent.

(a) short syllables have short vowels;
(b) long syllables have either long vowels *or* a diphthong; *or* a short vowel followed by two consonants;
(c) in words with long *and* short syllables the stress falls on the nearest *long* syllable to the end of the word;
(d) otherwise the stress is on the first syllable.

Examples: mu'Haṁmad; bayróot; ána.

3 **Intonation** One of the principal features distinguishing Levantine dialects one from another, and all from English, is the *intonation*, the rise and fall of the voice. Students should note different intonation patterns most carefully. A wrong intonation pattern is another common feature of a foreign accent.

4 **Junction and elision** The student should note how words 'run together', in order to avoid sounding too foreign.

A hyphen is intruded as a guide to pronunciation as follows: between /s/ and /h/ when these symbols represent separate consonants, for example, 'as-hal (easy). Therefore when /sh/ is written with no hyphen the sound is as in English *ship*. Similarly for *k-h/kh*, *t-h/th*, *d-h/dh* and *g-h/gh*.

An asterisk (*) in the table below indicates that the pronunciation of Levantine Arabic (in one or other dialect) may differ markedly from that of classical Arabic.

Please note

For most occurrences in classical Arabic of the unvoiced uvular plosive (*qaaf*: /q/ in transliteration) the symbol /'/ is used (i.e. the symbol for the glottal stop). Most Levantine dialects regularly make this 'conversion' from classical Arabic, but the student should note that:

1 Bedouin throughout the area use /g/ for /q/,
2 the Druzes systematically maintain /q/,
3 certain words always retain the classical /q/: *al-qur'aan* (Koran) and *al-qaahira* (Cairo).

Serial	Arabic letter	Name of letter	Trans-literation of name	Trans-literation symbol	Phonetic remarks
*1	ء	همزة	hamza	'	Glottal stop. In coll. A. often becomes lengthening of adjacent vowel: *ra's* becomes *raas*.
2	ب	باء	baa'	b	Voiced bilabial plosive.
3	ت	تاء	taa'	t	Dental, not alveolar as in English.
*4	ث	ثاء	thaa'	th	As in *thin*; in coll. A. often /t/ or /s/.
*5	ج	جيم	jeem	j	In Lebanon, often as in French *je*.
6	ح	حاء	Haa'	H	Notably strong expulsion of breath; unvoiced pharyngeal fricative.
7	خ	خاء	khaa'	kh	Rougher than in Scottish *loch*; unvoiced velar fricative.
8	د	دال	daal	d	Dental; not as in English /d/.
*9	ذ	ذال	dhaal	dh	As in *then*; frequently pron. /d/ or /z/ in coll. A.

Serial	Arabic letter	Name of letter	Trans-literation of name	Trans-literation symbol	Phonetic remarks
10	ر	راء	raa'	r	A much more trilled /r/ than in BRP.
11	ز	زاى	zay	z	More tense than in English z. In CA 14 often becomes /z/.
12	س	سين	seen	s	More tension and lip-spreading than in English sit.
13	ش	شين	sheen	sh	More tense than in English shop.
14	ص	صاد	Saad (cf. 12)	S	14–17 share the phonetic feature (velarization, pharyngealization)
15	ض	ضاد	Daad (cf. 8)	D	
16	ط	طاء	Taa' (cf. 3)	T	of Emphasis, and 17 has variant pronunciations.
*17	ظ	ظاء	Zaa' (cf. 11)	Z	CA 17 frequently becomes coll. A. 15.
18	ع	عين	9ayn	9	Voiced pharyngeal fricative.
19	غ	غين	ghayn	gh	Voiced uvular fricative, and similar to a Parisian r sound.
20	ف	فاء	faa'	f	As in off, not of. More tense than English.
*21	ق	قاف	qaaf	q	Unvoiced uvular plosive; in many dialects changes to glottal stop, or hamza.
22	ك	كاف	kaaf	k	As in kid.
23	ل	لام	laam	l	'Clear' not 'dark' /l/, i.e. more dental.
24	م	ميم	meem	m	
25	ن	نون	noon	n	
26	ه‍	هاء	haa'	h	An 'English' /h/. Cf. 6 above.

Serial	Arabic letter	Name of letter	Trans- literation of name	Trans- literation symbol	Phonetic remarks
27	و	واو	waw	w	With tension and lip-rounding.
28	ي	ياء	yaa'	y	With tension and lip-spreading.

Vowels

29	ـَ	فتحة	fatHa	a	Many allophones, but frequently as in BRP *hat*.
30	ـِ	كسرة	kesra	i	As in *pin*.
31	ـُ	ضمة	Damma	u	As in BRP *put*, never as in BRP *putt*.

Long vowels

32		ألف طويلة	'alif Taweela	aa	As in BRP *heart*, but allophonic variations occur. See the following pronunciation exercises.
33	ي			ee	Cf. 28 above; as in BRP *bee*, but more tense and with more lip-spreading than in English.
34	ُو			oo	Cf. 27 above; as in *food*, but with greater tension, and protrusion and rounding of the lips.

Diphthongs

35	ي			ay	As in *hay*, but as many allophones exist as in English *hay*.
36	وَ			aw	As in *mow*, but with greater lip-rounding and protrusion; allophones occur, e.g. the *o* of German *Lohn*.

Serial	Arabic letter	Name of letter	Trans- literation of name	Trans- literation symbol	Phonetic remarks
37				o	As in German *Lohn*. (Found principally in final position as 3 m. sing. pronoun.)

Note The /l/ of 'al, the definite article, is assimilated to the following consonant (i.e. there is gemination) when the noun following 'al begins with any of these sounds: nos 3, 4, 8–17 inclusive, 23, 25 and frequently 5 in Lebanon. Thus al-salaam becomes as-salaam and so on. These are 'sun-letters'. The rest are 'moon-letters'.

Pronunciation exercises

These are taken from *proper names*, i.e. names of persons and places of relevance to the modern Arabic and Islamic worlds, and to the Levant. The tape recordings should be used freely.

saqaTra	qubruS
dimashq	SaaliH
Hasan	Husayn
sa9eed	su9ood
najeeb	tawfeeq
saleem	saalim
meekhaa 'eel	faaDil
kareem	baheej
'ibraaheem	fareed
wadee9	9abd un-naaSir
9abd us-salaam 9aarif	9abd ul-laTeef baghdaadee
'aHmad shuqayree	'aHmad 9abd ullah
muHammad 9abd us-salaam	9alee 9abd ul-laTeef
9abd ul-kareem qaasim	9abdul-Hakeem 9aamir
'ash-shaykh saalim 'aS-SabaaH	'ameer al-kooayt
maHmood 9abd ul-waaHid	noor ud-deen 9abd ul-haadee
SalaaH ud-deen 'al-ayyoobee (Saladin)	muSTafa kamaal
	naSree shams ud-deen
muHammad salmaan	fareed al-'aTrash
9uthmaan Husayn	maHmood 'al-haashimee
'iHsaan Saadiq	najaat 'aS-Sagheera

naaZim 'al-qudsee   fareed shawqee
sameera tawfeeq   9umar 'ash-shareef
'aHmad shawqee   Saa'ib salaam
muHammad 9abd ul-wahhaab   yaasir 9arafaat
kaamil 'al-'as9ad

HOW TO USE THE BOOK

Without a teacher

There are scores of possible ways of using a combination of the
Arabic text, the translation or key and the sound recording of the
Arabic, but among the possibilities are the following four step-by-
step procedures for exercises and dialogues:
1   Read the English; say the Arabic; hear the Arabic recording;
repeat the Arabic.
2   As 1 and then: play your own voice recording; play the Arabic;
correct where necessary.
3   Hear the Arabic recording (at any point, i.e. in random fashion);
write the translation; check and correct where necessary.
4   Use the recordings for memorizing vocabulary; test yourself by
covering up the Arabic version and saying the Arabic; check from
the recording.

All sections of text which are on the cassette are marked ■ in the
margin.

With a teacher

The teacher will want to use his own methods based on experience,
but the following suggestions may be useful.
1   Ten drills based on the sentences and dialogues: repetition; in-
flexion; replacement; restatement; completion; transposition;
expansion; contraction; transformation; integration. (See the
author's *Course in Colloquial Arabic*, Beirut, 1974, pp. 12–14.)

Of these, **transformation** is particularly valuable for Arabic; a
given sentence can be changed for tense, negativeness, positiveness,
interrogative etc.
2   **Random comprehension practice** The teacher may use the
Arabic of the dialogues or the exercises for rapid-fire testing of

comprehension (in random order, preferably) or for eliciting the correct response.

3 **Action and movement** The teacher may have the student(s) act out the dialogues with appropriate exits and entrances when necessary.

4 **Recapitulation** The student(s) may be asked to re-tell the story of the dialogues and the anecdote in Lesson sixteen.

5 **Vocabulary testing** This can be done Arabic–English or English–Arabic using the lists in each chapter or, at a later stage, the vocabularies at the end of the book.

PART ONE
THE LESSONS

LESSON ONE
NOUNS AND ADJECTIVES;
BASIC SENTENCES

FIRST, THE GOOD NEWS

Equational sentences (e.g. The teacher/he . . . is . . .)

You can communicate a great deal in perfectly correct Arabic (spoken and written) *without using a single verb*.

1   The present tenses of *to be* and *to have* are not in the form of conjugated verbs in Arabic (see Lesson two for *to have*). In fact there is no need normally to say *is/are*.

2   The negative is formed by using one word (mush) systematically for nouns, adjectives and adverbs.

3   The interrogative is formed by simply changing the intonation of the voice. Compare English: They are not here, Aren't they here?

Examples

Salim is here—saleem hawn
Salim is not here—saleem mush hawn
Is Salim here?—saleem hawn?
Is Salim not here?—saleem mush hawn?
Karim is Lebanese—kareem lubnaanee
Karim is not Lebanese—kareem mush lubnaanee
Is Karim Lebanese?—kareem lubnaanee?
Is Karim not Lebanese?—kareem mush lubnaanee?

Note The 'Karim' sentences illustrate that all adjectives may be used as nouns. Indeed the classical grammarians say that the whole of Arabic grammar may be summed up in three parts: nouns, verbs and particles.

SUBJECT PRONOUNS

	Singular	*Plural*
1 c.	'ana	'iHna
2 m.	'inta	'intoo
2 f.	'intee	'intoo
3 m.	huwa	hum
3 f.	hiya	hum

Note (1) You and I—'ana oo 'inta. (2) Many dialects use a different compound form of the subject pronouns (see below, in Lesson two, 'Possession'): You and I—'ana oo iyyaak.

Examples

They are Jordanians—hum 'urdunee-een
We are Syrians—'iHna sooree-een
They are the Lebanese girls—hum 'il-banaat il-lubnaanee-een

AGREEMENT

Adjectives and verbs agree in gender and number with their noun or pronoun subjects in Arabic. *On the other hand . . .*
1   There is no indefinite article, let alone a declined one as in many European languages.
2   The definite article does not change for gender or number.
3   Plural non-humans are regarded as feminine singular for the purposes of grammatical agreement.

GENDER

The feminine adjective is formed in most cases by simply adding /a/: *shaikh, shaikha; sulTaan, sulTaana; lubnaanee, lubnaaneea; urdunee, urduneea.*

Adjectives formed from names, such as *lubnaan/lubnaanee*, *bay-root/bayrootee*, are called *nisba* adjectives (meaning *relationship*). When made feminine (by adding /*a*/) they double the /*ee*/ sound. The feminine *nisba* ending will henceforth be transcribed *-iyya*.

Noun	*Adjective*	*Feminine adjective*
lubnaan	lubnaanee	lubnaaniyya
bayroot	bayrootee	bayrootiyya
dimashq	dimashqee	dimashqiyya

Examples

The boy is Syrian—'il-walad sooree
The girl is Syrian—'il-bint sooriyya
The boy is a Muslim—'il-walad muslim
The girl is a Muslim—'il-bint muslima
Conversely, most nouns ending in /*a*/ are feminine.

NUMBER

1   Arabic has a form for *dual* (two of anything) formed by adding *-ayn* (as in Bahrain, Alamain etc.):

The two boys are here—'il-waladayn hawn
The two girls are here—'il-bintayn hawn

2   The most common plural formula (the 'sound' one) is that composed of the adjective/noun plus *-een*:

a Syrian—sooree (NB *no indefinite article in Arabic*)
the Syrians—'is-sooree-een

(Plurals formed otherwise – see Vocabulary – are called broken plurals.)
3   In colloquial Arabic the feminine plural ending (*-aat*) is not extensively used:

The girls are Syrian—'il-banaat sooree-een

4   The attributive adjective (e.g. 'the Syrian girls') must also be definite:

the Jordanian girls—'il-banaat 'il-'urdunee-een

5 Usually a dual noun (especially with humans) will, in colloquial Arabic, have a plural adjective:

the two Lebanese girls—'il-bintayn 'il-lubnaanee-een

THE *IDAFA* OR CONSTRUCT

This feature of Arabic has no equivalent in English, but the rules can be learned from simple, well-known examples.

The Arabic name Dar es Salaam means 'the abode of peace'. Notice that the first definite article is not used.

Rule 1 in the structure *the . . . of the . . .* the first definite article is not found:

the book of the boy—kitaab 'il-walad

Rule 2 the construct, if longer, removes all but the final definite article:

the book of the son of the teacher—kitaab 'ibn il-mu9allim

Rule 3 there is no 'apostrophe s' in Arabic. 'The boy's book' must be rendered 'the book of the boy'.

■ **VOCABULARY**

Arab—9arabee (*pl.* 9arab)
boy, son—walad (*pl.* 'awlaad)
son—'ibn (*pl.* 'abnaa)
girl, daughter—bint (*pl.* banaat)
ambassador—safeer (*pl.* sufaraa')
teacher—mu9allim (*pl.* -een)
book—kitaab (*pl.* kutub)
Lebanese—lubnaanee (*pl.* -een)
Syrian—sooree, shaamee (*pl.* -een)
Jordanian—'urdunee (*pl.* -een)
Palestinian—filisTeenee (*pl.* -een)
French—faransaawee (*pl.* -een)
English—'ingleezee (*pl.* 'ingleez)
American—'amreekaanee (*pl.* 'amreekaan)
foreigner—'ajnabee (*pl.* 'ajaanib)

■ **EXERCISE**

Translate:

1   'il-walad 'ingleezee
2   'il-bint faransiyya
3   'il-kitaab kitaab 9arabee
4   kitaab il-bint hawn
5   bint 'il-mu9allim hawn
6   The boy's teacher is a foreigner
7   The foreigner's sons are here
8   The American boy is the son of the teacher
9   We are the sons of the English teacher
10   The Syrian girl is the daughter of the ambassador

Make the above negative and/or interrogative, where feasible.

■ **DIALOGUE: East meets west**

A   marHaba!
B   marHabtayn! kayf 'il-Haal?
A   'il-Hamdu lillaah! kayf 'il-Haal?
B   il-Hamdu lillaah! 'inta ingleezee?
A   na9am 'ana ingleezee oo huwa amreekaanee
B   'ahlan wa sahlan!
A   'ahlan wa sahlan feek!

Translation

A   Hullo!
B   Hullo! how are you?
A   Praise be to God! How are you (How is the state)?
B   Praise be to God! Are you English?
A   Yes, I'm English and he is an American
B   Welcome!
A   *(Ritual reply implying that the welcome is embodied in the person extending it!)*

PROVERB

'il-walad walad wa law Hakam balad—Boys will be boys . . . (lit. 'The boy is a boy even though he rules a country!')

LESSON TWO
POSSESSION AND PRONOUNS

POSSESSION

1   The verb *to have* (present tense) is expressed in Arabic by saying that something is *with/to/in the possession of* someone.

I have a book—9indee kitaab
They have a book—9indhum kitaab

9ind implies *with/in the possession of/chez* etc. The pronouns attached to it have multiple uses: as possessive pronouns, object pronouns and as additions to prepositions.
   The full table is:

	Singular	*Plural*
1 c.	-ee (-nee *when object of verb and following prep.* fee)	-naa
2 m.	-ak	-kum (*or* koo)
2 f.	-ik	-kum (*or* koo)
3 m.	-o	-hum
3 f.	-ha	-hum

2   The negative is as follows:

I do not have a book—maa 9indee kitaab
Hasn't she a book?—maa 9indhaa kitaab?

3   my book—kitaabee
their books—kutubhum (*etc.*)

Note My book = the book of me. The definite article disappears, as this is a kind of *idafa* or construct. Attributive adjectives added to *my book* etc. must be definite.

my new book—kitaabee il-jadeed
her Arabic book—kitaabhaa il-9arabee

Note also A refinement is introduced for nouns ending in /a/ (see Vocabulary note below).

OTHER PRONOUN USES

1   you and I—'ana oo 'inta

In many Levantine dialects, however, this becomes *'ana oo 'iyyaak*; i.e. the possessive pronoun is added to *'iyyaa*.

we and they—'iHna oo 'iyyaahum

(In such phrases, pronoun order is always 1, 2 3; for example: you and they—inta oo iyyaahum.)

2   Added to prepositions:

from—min
with—ma9a
in—fee
from/with/in them—minhum/ma9hum/feehum

Note from/with/in me—minnee/ma9ee/feenee

3   Idiomatic expressions (m. and f.):

How are you?—kayfak? kayfik?
How are you? (Syria)—shlawnak? shlawnik?
(lit. 'What is your colour?')
Where are you?—waynak? waynik?
(often means 'How could you say/do such a thing?')

4   Objects of verbs. The pronouns are suffixed to verbs as direct or indirect objects (see Lesson three).
5   With *kull* (all), and other words:

all of us—kullnaa
all of them—kullhum
all/the whole of it—kullo

■ VOCABULARY

new—jadeed (*pl.* judud) (*often becomes* 'ijdeed, *pl.* 'ijdaad)
from—min
please—min faDlak (*lit. 'of your graciousness'*)
with—ma9
in—fee
house—bayt (*pl.* buyoot)

school—madrasa (*f.; pl.* madaaris)
large, big—kabeer (*pl.* kibaar)
small, young—Sagheer (*pl.* Sighaar) (*often becomes* 'iZgheer, *pl.*
  'iZghaar)
car—sayyaara (*f.; pl.* -aat)
man—rajul (*pl.* rijaal)
woman—mara (*f.; pl.* niswaan)
room—ghurfa (*f.; pl.* ghuraf)
yes—na9am
no—laa

Note on possessive pronouns

When a possessive pronoun or a noun 'in construct' is added to a
word ending in /a/ such as *sayyaara* (car), a /t/ is inserted before the
pronoun:

my car—sayyaaratee
the car of the teacher—sayyaarat 'il-mu9allim

(This is the *taa' marbooTa* of classical Arabic.)

■ **EXERCISE**

Translate:

1 huwa fee ghurfat 'il-mu9allim
2 'il-bintayn ma9a mu9allimee
3 'ir-rajul 'il-kabeer min 9ammaan
4 9indee bintayn oo walad
5 9indhaa kitaabha 'il-jadeed
6 He has a new car
7 She is with him in the large room
8 They are all with us here
9 All of us are English
10 All of them are foreigners
Make the above negative and/or interrogative, where feasible.

■ **DIALOGUE: Family news**

A 'ahlan wa sahlan!
B 'ahlan wa sahlan feek! kayf Haalak?

A 'il-Hamdu lillaah! kayfak inta?
B 'il-Hamdu lillaah! min faDlak, 9indak awlaad?
A na9am 9indee waladayn oo bint
B 'il-waladayn fil-madrasa?
A laa! hum Sighaar

Translation

A Welcome!
B And to you! (Approximately) 'How are you?'
A Praise be to God! How are *you*?
B Praise be to God! Please (i.e. excuse me for asking), do you have children?
A Yes, I have two boys and a girl
B Are the (two) boys in school?
A No, they are (too) young

PROVERB

haadha min faDl rabbee—This is by the graciousness of my Lord . . .

This sign, in classical Arabic, is frequently found as an inscription at the entrance to a house or other building.

■ APPENDIX NUMBERS

Connoisseurs have long savoured Tritton's despairing remark in *Teach Yourself Arabic* (London, 1943), 'The numerals are the nightmare of a bankrupt financier' (p. 171). Things are not quite so bad in colloquial Arabic.

1	waaHid (*f*. waaHida)	5	khamsa
2	'itnayn (*f*. tintayn)	6	sitta
3	talaata	7	sab9a
4	'arba9a	8	tamaanya

9	tis9a	15	khamst9ash(ar)
10	9ashara	16	sitt9ash(ar)
11	'iHd9ash(ar)	17	sab9at9ash(ar)
12	'itn9ash(ar)	18	tamaant9ash(ar)
13	talatt9ash(ar)	19	tis9at9ash(ar)
14	'arba9att9ash(ar)	20	9ishreen

Note

1 The 'intrusive' /t/ in 13–19 inclusive.
2 3–10 inclusive take a plural noun.
3 11 upwards take a singular noun (but see below at *Dates, times etc.*).
4 11–19 take final /-ar/ when followed by a noun.

Examples

Three men—talaata rijaal
Five women—khams niswaan

The classical Arabic rule of masculine numeral with feminine noun (and vice versa) is not closely observed in colloquial Arabic:

Sixteen books—sitt9ashar kitaab
Nineteen girls—tis9at9ashar bint

30	talaateen	70	sab9een
40	'arba9een	80	tamaaneen
50	khamseen	90	tis9een
60	sitteen	100	miyya

Examples

Thirty-five books (5 + 30)—khams oo talaateen kitaab
Sixty-four dollars (4 + 60)—'arba9a oo sitteen doolar

200	miyyatayn	900	tis9amiyya
300	talaatmiyya	1,000	'alf (*pl.* 'aalaaf)
400	'arba9amiyya	2,000	'alfayn
500	khamsmiyya	3,000	talaataalaaf
600	sittmiyya	6,000	sittaalaaf
700	sab9amiyya	10,000	9asharataalaaf
800	tamaanmiyya	20,000	9ishreen 'alf

Dates, times, etc.

1979 (books)—'alf oo tis9amiyya oo tis9a oo sab9een (kitaab) (NB *singular*)

1910 (books)—'alf oo tis9amiyya oo 9ashara (kutub) (NB *plural*)

the year 1945—sanat 'alf oo tis9a miyya oo khams oo 'arba9een

4 o'clock—is-saa9a 'arba9a

10.00—is-saa9a 9ashara

10.20—is-saa9a 9ashara oo tult (*a third*)

10.15—is-saa9a 9ashara oo rub9

10.30(35)—is-saa9a 9ashara oo nuSS (oo khamsa)

10.45—is-saa9a 'iHd9ashar illaa rub9 (*i.e.* 11−¼)

2.00—is-saa9a tintayn (*in some dialects*)

Telephone numbers are frequently divided as follows:

123456—(123 / 456) miyya oo talaata oo 9ishreen (*pause*) 'arba9 miyya oo sitta oo khamseen

THERE IS/ARE

fee (indeclinable) renders both *there is* and *there are*. The negative is *maa fee*. In some dialects /-sh/ is suffixed. In some dialects this /-sh/ is a common suffix added to *all verbs* for negation. For example:

I have not—maa 9indeesh

VOCABULARY

everyone—kull waaHid

day—yawm (*pl.* 'ayyaam)

week—'usboo9 (*pl.* 'asaabee9) (*from* sab9a, *seven*)

month—shahr (*pl.* shuhoor)

year—sana (*pl.* sineen *or* sanawaat)

minute (n.)—da'ee'a (*pl.* da'aayi')

hour—saa9a (*pl.* -aat)

either . . . or, or—yaa . . . yaa; 'aw

How much/many? (followed by sing.)—kam? 'addaysh?

age—9umr (*pl.* 'a9maar)

■ **EXERCISE**

Translate:

1   kam 'usboo9 fee fis-sana?
2   fee miyya oo 9ishreen da'ee'a fee saa9atayn
3   kam 9umro? 9umro sitta shuhoor
4   9umr il-walad 9ashar sineen
5   In the Islamic calendar (*hijree*) month there are twenty-nine or thirty days
6   9indo 9ishreen kitaab
7   9indhum 'arba9a sayyaaraat
8   ma9ee talaateen leera sooree
9   ma9haa khams oo 'arba9een deenaar 'urdunee
10   sanat 'alf oo tis9amiyya oo 'arba9t9ash
11   I have 3 new cars
12   She has 53 Lebanese lira (with her)
13   Have you got 33 Jordanian dinars (on you)?
14   (Telephone) 459/937
15   the year 1939

Give 6–9 above in the negative where feasible.

LESSON THREE
VERBS, WORD ORDER
AND DEMONSTRATIVES

VERBS: INTRODUCTION

Strong men have been known to blench at the thought of conjugating verbs; *any* verbs, let alone Arabic ones. Moreover the published memoirs of old-Arab-world hands are replete with heart-rending accounts of grappling in Aden or Lebanon (without benefit of air-conditioning and heating respectively) with the forty-four (or was it ninety-two?) forms of the verbal noun.

There *are* difficulties, but the reader may be assured that the Arabic verb system is much easier to grasp than that of Russian,

German or French, and is simplicity itself compared to the English. Not for Arabic speakers the deviousness of the (British) English 'I should've thought . . .', meaning 'I think, and contradiction is inconceivable'. Arabic is by comparison the soul of economy and elegance, in form and function.

First the bad news

– Arabic verbs conjugate for number and gender (classical Arabic verbs have thirteen 'persons': singular, dual and plural).
– In addition to indulging in fancies such as hollow verbs, assimilated verbs, doubly defective verbs and quadriliteral verbs, Arabic is prolific in derived forms of the same, viz. Forms II to XV.
– For the 'simple' verb there are forty-four patterns possible for the verbal noun.

Now the good news

– Colloquial Arabic has no dual form in verb conjugation.
– The distinction between plural masculine and feminine is neutralized: i.e. there is only one form for each of *we*, *you* and *they* (dual masculine and feminine; plural masculine and feminine).
– Arabic has only two tenses: past and non-past.
– The past tense is formed by adding suffixes.
– The non-past is formed by adding prefixes (plus some of the 'past' suffixes to indicate number).
– Prefixes and suffixes are standard for all types of verb.
There is almost no such thing as an irregular verb in Arabic.
– The subject of the verb if a pronoun (*I/we* etc.) is included in the subject; pronouns are used only to give extra emphasis.
– The economy of prefixes/suffixes used is extreme: the foreigner often feels there is risk of ambiguity. For example:

I/you (m. sing.) wrote—katab/t/
you (m. sing.)/she writes—ta/ktub

– The prefixes and suffixes are nearly all clearly related to the subject/possessive pronouns (see Lessons one and two). For example:

you (f. sing.) wrote—katab/tee (*cf.* in/tee: *you f. sing.*)
you (pl.) wrote—katab/too (*cf.* 'in/too: *you pl.*)

– Negation of verbs is done in only one way in colloquial Arabic: the word *maa* is placed immediately before *all* forms of the verb (classical Arabic has one form for past (*maa*) and another for non-past (*laa*), a distinction more or less suppressed in colloquial Arabic).

– The interrogative form is nearly always achieved by simply changing the intonation of the affirmative form.

– Derived forms in colloquial Arabic are nine only, not II–XV as in classical Arabic.

To sum up

As with reports of Mark Twain's death, reports of the difficulty of Arabic verbs have been greatly exaggerated.

CONJUGATION OF PAST TENSE OF SIMPLE VERBS

he wrote—katab

Note In Arabic grammar the starting point is always *he*, not the infinitive as in European languages (*to write* etc.).

	Singular	*Plural*
1 c.	I—katabt	we—katabnaa
2 m.	you—katabt	you—katabtoo
2 f.	you—katabti	you—katabtoo
3 m.	he—katab	they—kataboo
3 f.	she—katabat	they—kataboo

Note The above is the *active voice*. The passive (It was written) is little used in colloquial: either *They wrote it* or Form VII (see below, *Derived forms of verbs*) is used.

Exercise

Conjugate the following verbs:

open, *fataH*; eat, *'akal*; return, come back, *raja9*; drink, *sharib*; know, *9araf*; do, make, *9amil*; take, *'akhad*; go up, *Tala9*; go down, *nazal*; ask, *sa'al*

OBJECT PRONOUNS

The object pronouns (see Lesson two) are suffixed to verbs:

He wrote it—katabo
She knew them—9arafat -hum

Note When *it/him* (*o*) is added to verbs ending in a long vowel, the pronoun is indicated simply by lengthening the final vowel (indicated below by (h)):

You (f. sing.) wrote it—katabtee(h)
They ate it—'akaloo(h)

WORD ORDER

Classical Arabic prefers the order: verb + subject + predicate. For example: wrote + The boys + letters. Furthermore, in such cases the verb is always singular.

Colloquial Arabic prefers the order: subject + verb + predicate.

The boys wrote letters—'il-'awlaad kataboo makaateeb

i.e. the verb agrees in gender and number with its subject.

NEGATION AND INTERROGATION

Negation

The rule is very simple: the verb takes *maa*, immediately preceding.

The boys did not write letters—'il-'awlaad maa kataboo makaateeb

Interrogative form

This is indicated by changing the intonation. Occasionally a classical Arabic form (*hal*) is used, particularly when a speaker wishes to upstage his interlocutor. (Arabic has many devices to be used as conversation-stoppers or to focus the attention of the speaker. See Lesson fourteen on *Proverbs*.)

Did they write letters?—hal kataboo makaateeb?

DERIVED FORMS OF VERBS

Introduction (Past tense)

This section concentrates on the aspects of conjugation, meaning-survey and usage. Like the man who discovered he had been speaking prose all his life, the student may be pleasantly surprised to find he has been using Arabic derived-form verbs without being a master of the contents of Wright's *Arabic Grammar* (2 vols, 3rd edn, Cambridge, 1964).

Conjugation

All forms except IX (see Lesson seven below) are conjugated exactly like the verbs in the previous section of this chapter. For example:

from he knew—9araf
comes they became acquainted (with)—ta9arrafoo (9ala)
This is a Form V verb.

Below are some specimen verbs:

Form II	send someone/thing back	rajja9
	(*from* come back	raja9)
III	correspond with someone	kaatab
	(*from* write	katab)
IV	send someone/thing down	'anzal
	(*from* go down	nazal)
V	become acquainted (with)	ta9arraf (9ala)
	(*from* know	9araf)
VI	become acquainted with each other	ta9aaraf
	(*from* know	9araf)
VII	be written	'inkatab
	(*from* write	katab)
VIII	be assembled	'ijtama9
	(*from* gather, add	jama9)
X	use, employ	'ista9mal
	(*from* do, make	9amil)

Survey of meaning and usage

The **forms** of verbs are completely consistent: Form VII verbs always put /'in/ before the Form I verb; Form V verbs always double the middle radical of Form I verbs and put /ta/ before the result (which, itself, is the form for Form II verbs); and so on.
Exercise: form the derived forms of *fa9al*.

Meaning is not quite so consistent: hence the many academic jokes about the meaning of Arabic derived-form verbs. However, in general the following guide is true, though not the whole truth.

Form II   often means to make someone do the action of Form I: hence *rajja9* means 'to make someone/thing go back', i.e. 'to send back'.

Form III   frequently means to do the action of Form I to someone: hence *kaatab* means 'to write to someone'. (Lots of academic jokes here on the sexual proclivities of Form III verbs. And in fact the verb 'to have sexual intercourse with (a woman)' is a Form III verb.)

Form IV   often has the same meaning as Form II. Both *nazzal* (II) and *'anzal* (IV) mean 'to make go down' (e.g. to drop off passengers from a cab). (*'anzal* means also 'to send down the revelation', i.e. reveal the Koran.) **Note** IV frequently has a 'denominative' meaning. For example *'aslam* means 'to become a Muslim'.

Form V   usually the passive of II. *9arraf* (II) means 'to make someone know someone' (i.e. introduce someone to someone else), so *ta9arraf* (V) (*9ala*) means 'to be introduced (to) someone'.

Form VI   usually the reflexive of III: hence *ta9aarafoo* means 'they got to know one another'.

Form VII   in Levantine Arabic a heavily used form, by comparison with other dialects. It is most commonly used in place of the passive. Where other dialects use the passive or the form 'They did so-and-so', Levantine Arabic generates Form VII verbs. From the verbs in the previous section come: be opened, *infataH*; be edible, *'in'akal*; be drinkable, *'insharib*; be known, *'in9araf*; be done, *'in9amal*.

Form VIII   frequently the passive of Form I. *jama9* = gather, add; *'ijtama9* = be gathered, assembled.

Form X   has possibly the most diverse collection of areas of meaning attaching to it, some only vaguely related: hence yet more academic jokes. Frequently has a sense of 'to make something perform the action of Form I'. Hence *ista9mal* means 'to make something work', i.e. 'employ'. (Form IX, by the way, is used only for colours and defects in classical Arabic, and in colloquial Arabic almost solely for colours: e.g. *'iHmarr* means 'to become red', from *'ahmar*, red. See Lesson seven below.)

DEMONSTRATIVES (this, that, these, etc.)

		Singular	*Plural*
this	m.	haada	haadol
	f.	haadi	haadol
that	m.	haadaak	haadolak
	f.	haadeek	haadolik (*or as above*)

The above are the pronoun forms.

This is a book—haada kitaab
These are foreigners—haadol 'ajaanib
Note This is the book—haadal-kitaab

(The intonation indicates that this is a sentence with a predicate in the definite form. The first syllable in the sentence is more stressed than usual.)
When used as adjectives all forms of *this* can be replaced by *hal*. For example:

These boys are Lebanese—hal-'awlaad lubnaanee-een

In Lebanon, especially, a double-demonstrative is frequently used.

this book—hal-kitaab haada (hayy)

■ VOCABULARY

newspaper—jareeda (*pl.* jaraayid)
door, gate—baab (*pl.* 'abwaab)

water—mayy (*f.*; *pl.* -aat)
map—khaarTa (*pl.* kharaayiT)
to (prep.)—'ila
Who?—meen?
When?—'aymta?
on—9ala
chair—kursee (*pl.* karaasee)

Verbs

write—katab
arrive—waSal
correspond with (someone)—kaatab
open; opened—fataH; maftooH
be opened—'infataH
eat—'akal
return, come back—raja9
send back—rajja9
drink—sharib
know—9araf
get to know, be introduced to . . .—ta9arraf 9ala . . .
get to know each other—ta9aaraf
do, make—9amil
be done—'in9amal
employ, use—ista9mal
take—'akhad
go up—Tala9
go down—nazal
send down, put down—nazzal (*or* 'anzal)
ask—sa'al

■ **EXERCISE**

Translate:

1 'akhadoo ma9hum miyya oo talaateen jareeda
2 meen fataH hal-baab?
3 'aymta ta9arrafti 9ala hal-kitaab?
4 'awlaad il-madrasa ista9maloo kharaayiT
5 'il-'ajaanib nazaloo min 9ammaan ila 'areeHa (Jericho)

6 This is the map of Damascus
7 He took all of them with him to Beirut
8 They sent every one of us back from Damascus to Amman
9 They took the chairs from our school
10 I wrote to him in 1958

Make the above negative and/or interrogative where possible.
Substitute other subjects for the verbs above (they for he, etc.).

■ **DIALOGUE: A safe return**

A   'ahlan! marHaba! kayf Haalak?
B   marHabtayn! il-Hamdu lillaah! kayf il-Haal?
A   il-Hamdu lillaah! 'aymta waSalt min 9ammaan?
B   'abl saa9atayn
A   il-Hamdu lillaah 'is-salaama!
B   'allaah yisallimak!

Translation

A   Hullo! Welcome! How are you?
B   Hullo! Praise be to God! How are you?
A   Praise be to God! When did you arrive from Amman?
B   Two hours ago.
A   Praise be to God for your safety!
B   God bless you!

PROVERB

'ibnak 'inta mitlak inta—Like father like son

LESSON FOUR
VERBS, CONJUNCTIONS
AND ELATIVES

VERBS: NON-PAST, SIMPLE AND DERIVED FORMS

From he wrote — katab

Formation

The radicals retain their position throughout (k–t–b), the vowelling is changed (more or less systematically) and the prefixes (and suffixes) added to indicate the subject are mostly related to pronouns already learned.

	Singular	*Plural*
1 c.	/'a/ktub ('ana)	/na/ktub ('iHna)
2 m.	/ta/ktub ('inta)	/ta/ktub/oo ('intoo)
2 f.	/ta/ktub/ee/ ('intee)	/ta/ktub/oo ('intoo)
3 m.	yaktub	/ya/ktub/oo
3 f.	/ta/ktub	/ya/ktub/oo/

Anyone knowing classical Arabic will recognize the similarity to colloquial Arabic forms. The above forms *are* used in colloquial Arabic, for example following auxiliary verbs (such as *must*, *laazim*; *may*, *mumkin*) but in the Levant two changes are made to the above.

1 Where *u* is the vowel before the third radical, *u* is most frequently used also before the first radical: i.e. there is regressive vowel harmony: *yaktub* becomes *yuktub*. (Bear this in mind for the imperative form below.)

2 Before the prefixes mentioned above, a bilabial (unreleased) is added, which is /b/ in all forms except 1 plural, where it is /m/.

	Singular	*Plural*
1 c.	(b)uktub	(m)nuktub
2 m.	(b)tuktub	(b)tuktuboo
2 f.	(b)tuktubee	(b)tuktuboo
3 m.	(b)yuktub	(b)yuktuboo
3 f.	(b)tuktub	(b)yuktuboo

Meaning and extensions

1 The non-past form, above, means

He is writing, he writes—byuktub

Also, 'he does write' (but see present continuous, at 7 below)

2 He will write—raaH yuktub

(**Note** raaH does not change for number or gender. After most auxiliary verbs the non-past has no /b/ or /m/ prefix.)

3 We must write—laazim nuktub

Note We must not write—mush laazim nuktub

(Again: *laazim* is invariable and the non-past verb has no /b/ or /m/ prefix.)

4 He wants to write—biddo yuktub (*bidd* + pronouns + verb without *b/m*)

5 They may write—mumkin yuktuboo
(i.e. 'possibly')

6 We can write—feenaa nuktub

(The preposition *fee* ('in') takes the normal pronoun suffixes and comes to mean 'it is in my power/ability':

Note I can—feenee)

7 **Present continuous**

I am/We are (etc.) writing—9am buktub (*especially in Lebanon and Syria*)

Non-past conjugation (continued)

Take the verbs used in Lesson three and note their non-past form

	Past	*Non-past*
open	fataH	byiftaH
eat	'akal	byaakul
return	raja9	byirja9

	Past	*Non-past*
drink	sharib	byishrab
know	9araf	bya9rif
do, make	9amil	byi9mal
take	'akhad	byaakhud
go up	Tala9	byiTla9
go down	nazal	byinzal
ask	sa'al	byis'al

Exercise

Conjugate the above fully in the present continuous.

Some rules may be derived from the above as to the final vowels used, but from the learner's point of view it is just as easy to learn each verb, in the past and non-past, as *one item*. Henceforth verbs will be given in this form, for example:

write—katab, byuktub

Derived forms non-past: conjugation

Here there is a completely systematic formation:

		Past	*Non-past*
II	send back	rajja9	byirajji9
III	correspond with	kaatab	byikaatib
IV	send down	'anzal	byinzil
V	get to know	ta9arraf	byita9arraf
VI	get to know each other	ta9aaraf	byita9aaraf
VII	be opened	'infataH	byinfatiH
VIII	be assembled	'ijtama9	byijtami9
X	use	'ista9mal	byista9mil

Rules

1   All derived-form verbs behave this way.
2   In the non-past the final vowel before the third radical is always /i/, except in V and VI where it is always /a/.

3 In the non-past the distinguishing feature of the past tense is preserved, i.e. the /aa/ of Form III, the second-radical doubling of V and VI, etc.

THE IMPERATIVE (positive and negative)

This is formed from the non-past:

	Non-past	*Imperative*
write	byuktub	'uktub!
open	byiftaH	'iftaH!
return	byirja9	'irja9!
drink	byishrab	'ishrab!
do, make	byi9mal	'9mal!
go up	byiTla9	'iTla9!
go down	byinzil	'inzil!
ask	byis'al	'is'al!

Formation

1 Remove the /b/ and prefix (e.g. *byu-*).
2 Replace by the vowel /u/ when final vowel is /u/; otherwise replace by /i/.
3 Feminine: add suffix /ee/. Plural: add suffix /oo/.

	Masculine singular	*Feminine*	*Plural (m. and f.)*
write	'uktub!	'uktubee!	'uktuboo!

Note Two important exceptions:

eat	kul!	kulee!	kuloo!
take	khud!	khudee!	khudoo!

Negative imperative

Do not write!—maa *or* laa tuktub (/ee/, /oo/)

Rule

Take the non-past 2 m. sing. (without the /b/ prefix) and place before it *maa* or *laa* (this applies to derived-form verbs also).

Exercise

Negate the eight imperatives listed above.

Derived-form imperative (positive: see above for negative)

Again these are completely systematic and predictable

Non-past	*Imperative*
byirajji9	rajji9!
byikaatib	kaatib!
byinzil	'anzil!
byita9arraf	ta9arraf!
byita9aaraf	ta9aaraf!
byinfatiH	'infatiH!
byijtami9	'ijtami9!
byista9mil	'ista9mil!

Rules

1 Remove the /byi/ prefix.
2 If the result begins with a single consonant that is the imperative.
3 Where the result begins with two consonants add a vowel: /a/ for Form IV, /i/ for Forms VII, VIII and X.

Exercise

Form the full imperative (masculine and feminine; singular and plural; positive and negative) of the following verbs:

Form	*Meaning*	*Arabic*	*Form I*
II	teach	9allam	(9alam)
III	consult	raaja9	(raja9)
IV	expel	'akhraj	(kharaj)
V	learn	ta9allam	(9alam)
VI	wonder, ask oneself	tasaa'al	(sa'al)
VII	(extremely rare in imperative)		
VIII	open (ceremonially)	iftataH	(fataH)
X	regain	'istarja9	(raja9)

CONJUNCTIONS

The particle *maa* (meaning 'the time when') is used to make conjunctions from prepositions.

Preposition	Meaning	Conjunction	Meaning
9ind	at	9indmaa	when
'abl	before	'ablmaa	before
ba9d	after	ba9dmaa	after

e.g. After he arrived I introduced him to the teacher—ba9dmaa waSal 9arrafto 9ala-l mu9allim

ELATIVES (comparatives and superlatives)

Possibly the two most powerful words in all Arabic, and indeed in all Islamic history:

God is Most Great!—allaahu 'akbar!

The pattern *'a/k/ba/r* is typical of all comparatives and superlatives (elative).

Adjective	Meaning	Elative form
kabeer	big	'akbar
Sagheer	small	'aSghar
kateer	much	'aktar
rakheeS	cheap	'arkhaS
Hasan	good	'aHsan

The elative without *'al-* is comparative.
The elative with *'al-* is superlative. (Al-Azhar, in Cairo, means 'the most resplendent'.)
Where radicals 2 and 3 are the same, note the formation:

jadeed	new	'ajadd
shadeed	intense	'ashadd
bigger than . . .		'akbar min . . .
She is bigger than I		hiyya 'akbar minnee

VOCABULARY

Review the vocabulary of the previous lessons, especially the verbs.

Note The tag-phrase equivalent to *n'est-ce pas* in French: *mush hayk* ('Is it not so?').

■ **EXERCISE**

Translate:

1 rajja9naa l-kutub 'abl-maa waSaloo
2 iftaH baab il-madrasa!
3 'uktub maktoob 'ila-l mu9allim!
4 9arrafna 9ala 'ibn is-safeer
5 hal-kitaab 'aHsan min haadaak, mush hayk?
6 They must introduce me to the boys at 4.30
7 Don't (pl.) write more than four letters!
8 He wrote his letters after we arrived
9 They want to write letters to their children
10 You (f. sing.) will drink water with your food (*'akl*)

Make the above feminine, plural, negative, interrogative, where feasible.

■ **DIALOGUE: Lost property**

A meen 'akhad il-karaasee min hal-ghurfa?
B 'ibraaheem akhad-hum 'abl saa9atayn, mush hayk?
A mush laazim yaakhud shee (*anything*) min hawn!
B Tayyib, 'urajji9hum ilal-ghurfa?
A na9am! rajji9hum, 'i9mal ma9roof!

Translation

A Who has taken the chairs from this room?
B Ibrahim took them two hours ago, didn't he?
A He should not take anything from here!
B OK, shall I bring them back to the room?
A Yes, please return them ('do (me) a favour')!

PROVERB

'akbar minnak bi-yawm 'a9lam minnak bi-sana—He who is one day older than you is one year more knowledgeable (*sic?*)

LESSON FIVE
PARTICIPLES

PARTICIPLES, ACTIVE AND PASSIVE

Form

The formation is quite systematic.

Form I verbs

	Active	Passive
write (katab)	kaatib (aa-i)	maktoob (ma––oo–)
open (fataH)	faatiH	maftooH
drink (sharib)	shaarib	mashroob
know (9alam)	9aalim	ma9loom

Derived-form verbs

II *teach* (9allam)   mu9*a*llim
(final/*i*/) (*teacher*)   mu9*a*llam (*final* /a/)

III *write to* (kaatab)
mukaat*i*b (*correspondent*)   mukaat*a*b

IV *expel* ('akhraj)   mukhr*i*j
(*producer*)   mukhr*a*j

V *learn* (ta9allam)
muta9all*i*m (*learned*)   muta9all*a*m

VI *wonder* (tasaa'al)
mutasaa'*i*l (*wondering*)   mutasaa'*a*l

VII *be open* (infataH)
munfat*i*H (*open-minded*)   munfat*a*H

VIII *gather, be assembled*
('ijtama9)   mujtam*i*9   mujtam*a*9
(*assembled*)

X *regain* ('istarja9)
mustarj*i*9   mustarj*a*9

40

Meaning and usage

Active participle

1 Normally this is the doer of the action. For example:

kaatib (*writer*); 9aalim (*scholar*); mu9allim (*teacher*); mukaatib (*correspondent*).

2 Sometimes, the active participle can mean that an action has been completed. For example:

Will you have something to drink?—btishrab shee?
No, thanks! I've had a drink—laa, shukran! 'ana shaarib

3 A common Levantine usage is:

He has just arrived—ba9do waaSil
We have just arrived—ba9dna waaSileen

(i.e. the preposition *ba9d* + pronouns + active participle, which is inflected for gender and number. Compare Irish–English 'He's (just) after coming').
4 *faatiH* can mean 'opened' (e.g. for shops).

Passive participle

1 In the strict sense of the passive participle – the action having been done:

It has been written—maktoob

(This expression is used to accept fate, in the sense that such-and-such an occurrence has been known to God forever.)
2 As a noun: *maktoob* ('a letter'). **Note** many such nouns have broken plurals.

letter maktoob *becomes* makaateeb, *but*
drink mashroob *becomes* mashroobaat

3 Some plural passive participles have no singular:

information—ma9loomaat
food—ma'koolaat

4 The passive participles of derived-form verbs can be used to

mean *the place of* an action. Thus, society (place of gathering together) is *mujtama9*.

hospital (place of seeking a cure)—mustashfa

■ **VOCABULARY**

Verbs

dwell, live—sakan, byuskun
hear—sami9, byisma9
be present—HaDar, byuHDur
prepare, make ready—HaDDar (II)
wear, put on (clothes)—labis, byilbas
study—daras, byudrus
close—sakkar (II)
enter—dakhal, byudkhul

Nouns

shop—dukkaan (*f.* dakaakeen)
office—maktab (*pl.* makaatib)
dwelling—maskan (*pl.* masaakin)
entrance—madkhal (*pl.* madaakhil)
exit—makhraj (*pl.* makhaarij)
street—shaari9 (*pl.* shawaari9)
clothes—malaabis

Adjectives

cold—baarid
present, 'there'—mawjood
first—'awwal
second (also 'other')—taanee
third—taalit
fourth—raabi9
fifth—khaamis
sixth—saadis
seventh—saabi9

eighth—taamin
ninth—taasi9
tenth—9aashir

(Note the pattern /aa–i/ imposed on the basic number *'arba9*: *raabi9*.)

Particles

What?—shoo?
Why?—laysh? lay?

■ **EXERCISE**

Translate:

1 intoo saakineen fish-shaari9 it-taanee, mush hayk?
2 HaDDir 'il-'akl, min faDlak!
3 9am byudrus khaarTat il-makaatib il-jadeeda
4 'udkhul oo sakkir il-baab!
5 laysh il-awlaad laabiseen malaabis 9arabiyya?
6 Take these letters to the office entrance at 2.30
7 He heard them before they entered
8 Are these shops open at 7.30?
9 We must drink something cold
10 They may possibly eat something before 4.45

Make the above negative, interrogative, feminine and plural where feasible.

■ **DIALOGUE: A phone call**

A allo!
B (*Caller*) ahlan! marHaba! kayf Haalak?
A il-Hamdu lillaah! kayfak inta?
B nushkur allaah! kayf il-'awlaad?
A mabsooTeen, byisallimoo 9alayk!
B allaah yisallimak! min faDlak, fu'aad mawjood?
A mush saami9. meen?
B fu'aad
A laa, fu'aad mush mawjood

B   mush haada arba9 oo khamseen talaat miyya oo talaata oo
     khamseen?
A   laa, Habeebee, ghalaT!

Translation

A   Hullo!
B   Welcome! How are you?
A   Praise be to God! How are you?
B   We thank God! How are the children?
A   Very well, and they send you their best wishes ('they greet you')
B   God bless you! Please, is Fuad there?
A   I can't hear (you). Who?
B   Fuad
A   No, Fuad's not here
B   Isn't this 54/353?
A   No, my dear (chap?) Wrong number!

Proverb

sakkir daarak, 'aamin jaarak—Lock your door (and only *then*) trust
your neighbour

LESSON SIX
HOLLOW VERBS AND
'TO BE ABLE'

HOLLOW VERBS

These verbs are so called because the middle radical is unstable: a
verb with /aa/ medial in the *past* may become /aa/, /ee/ or /oo/ in the
non-past, according to certain rules: *kaan* (he was) may be taken as
an example.

	Past	Non-past
3 m. sing.	kaan	byikoon
3 pl.	kaanoo	byikoonoo

When the middle radical is followed by two consonants, however, the /aa/ is shortened as follows: for verbs with /oo/ in the non-past /aa/ becomes /u/, otherwise it becomes /i/.

	Past	*Non-past*
2 m. sing.	ku/nt/	bitkoon
2 m. pl.	ku/nt/oo	bitkoonoo

Other types of hollow verbs

	Past	*Non-past*
3 m. sing.	khaaf (*fear*)	byikhaaf
2 m. sing.	khift	btkhaaf
3 m. sing.	Saar (*become*)	byiSeer
2 m. sing.	Sirt	btSeer

Past tense of kaan

	Singular	*Plural*
1 c.	kunt	kunna
2 m.	kunt	kuntoo
2 f.	kunti	kuntoo
3 m.	kaan	kaanoo
3 f.	kaanat	kaanoo

In other words, /aa/ is maintained *only* in all the third persons.

Exercise

Conjugate (past tense) *khaaf, byikhaaf* (fear); *naam byinaam* (sleep); *Saar byiSeer* (become); *Taar byiTeer* (fly).

Hollow verbs, non-past tense

Rule The appropriate long vowel is maintained throughout.

	Type 1	*Type 2*	*Type 3*
3 m. sing.	byikoon	byinaam	byiTeer
2 m. sing.	bitkoon	bitnaam	bitTeer
3 pl.	byikoonoo	byinaamoo	byiTeeroo

Participles

Active: khaayif, naayim, Saayir, Tayyir
Passive: almost non-existent

Exercise

Conjugate the above verbs fully.

KAAN AND VERBS (pluperfect and past continuous)

He had studied—kaan daras
We had studied—kunna darasna

Rule

The pluperfect of any verb is formed by *kaan* + verb (past tense, both verbs conjugating):

He was studying *or* He used to study—kaan yudrus

To emphasize *past continuity* many Levantine dialects use the particle of the present continuous, *9am* (see Lesson four).

He was studying—kaan 9am byudrus

HOLLOW VERBS, DERIVED FORMS

The second radical is maintained throughout in Forms II, III, V, and VI.

	Past	*Non-past*
II	Sawwar (*photograph*)	byiSawwir
III	saayar (*go along with, 'humour'*)	byisaayir
V	taSawwar (*imagine*)	byitaSawwar
VI	tashaawar (*consult each other*)	byitashaawar

In Forms IV, VII, VIII and X, the rule for shortening the vowel in the *past* is observed.

	Form IV	*VII*	*VIII*	*X*
3 m. sing.	'adaar	'inqaad	'irtaa'H	'istajaab
	(administer)	(be led)	(relax, rest)	(respond to)

	Form IV	*VII*	*VIII*	*X*
2 m. sing.	'ada/irt	'inqa(d/t)t	'irtaHt	'istaja/ibt

(*a/i* and *d/t* imply free variation)

Non-past tense:

3 m. sing.	byideer	byinqaad	byirtaaH	byistajeeb
2 m. sing.	bitdeer	btinqaad	btirtaaH	btistajeeb

(**Note** No derived-form hollow verb has /oo/ in the non-past.)

Exercise

Conjugate the above verbs fully.
Note Very useful hollow verbs:

Bring!—haat! (/ee/,/oo/)
(This verb is found only in the *imperative*.)

Take away!—sheel! (/ee/,/oo/)

IMPERATIVES

These are formed from the non-past, and always have the long vowel of the non-past.

	Past	*Non-past*	*Imperative*
go	raaH	byirooH	rooH! (/ee/, /oo/)
sleep	naam	byinaam	naam!
bring	jaab	byijeeb	jeeb!
see	shaaf	byishoof	shoof! (*'Look!'*)

Derived forms

Forms II, III, V and VI are quite regular:

		Past	*Non-past*	*Imperative*
II	photograph	Sawwar	byiSawwir	Sawwir!
III	consult	shaawar	byishaawir	shaawir!
V	imagine	taSawwar	byitaSawwar	taSawwar!
VI	consult each other	tashaawar	byitashaawar	tashaawar!

Forms IV, VII, VIII, X

IV	administer	adaar	byideer	'adeer!
VII	be led	inqaad	byinqaad	('inqaad!)
VIII	relax, rest	'irtaaH	byirtaaH	'irtaaH!
X	respond to	istajaab	byistajeeb	'istajeeb!

Note The imperative always has a long vowel in the above four forms.

Participles

Active: muSawwir (II), mushaawir (III), mudeer (IV), mutaSawwir (V), mutashaawir (VI), munqaad (VII), murtaaH (VIII), mustajeeb (X).

Passive: muSawwar (II), mushaawar (III), mudaar (IV), muta-Sawwar (V), (mutashaawar) (VI), (munqaad) (VII), (murtaaH) (VIII), (mustajaab) (X).

Note All active participles have /i/ or /ee/ finally. All passive participles have /a/ or /aa/ finally. Notice that in VII and VIII /aa/ distinguishes both forms, active and passive.

TO BE ABLE

Arabic has a distinction somewhat similar to that of French between *savoir* and *pouvoir*, though in Arabic there is more free variation. Two verbs are acceptable: *'adar, byi'dir*; and *9araf, byi9raf*. These are followed by another verb *always in the non-past* (with some exceptions in some dialects), with no *b/m-* prefix.

Can you write?—bta9rif tuktub? *or* bti'dir tuktub?
He could not write the letter—maa 'adar yuktub il-maktoob

◼ VOCABULARY

Verbs

take away—shaal, byisheel
go—raaH, byirooH
see—shaaf, byishoof
say, tell—'aal, byi'ool

bring—jaab, byijeeb
speak—takallam (V)
rise, get up—'aam, byi'oom

Nouns/adjectives

language—lugha (*pl.* -aat)
classical—faSeeH (*f.* fuSHa)
colloquial—daarij (*or* 9aammiyya)
table—Taawila (*pl.* -aat)
knife—sikkeen(a) (*usually f.*; *pl.* sakaakeen)
fork—shawka (*pl.* shuwak)
spoon—mal9a'a (*pl.* malaa9i')
today—il-yawm
tonight—il-layla

Particles

How?—kayf?
between, among—bayn
above—faw'
below—taHt
only, but—bass
a little—shwayy, 'aleel

■ **EXERCISE**

Translate:

1 baynee oo baynak, maa ta'ool shee il-layla!
2 bta9rif tatakallam 9arabee daarij?
3 laa, bass ba9rif 'uktub 9arabee
4 rooH, shoof shughlak!
5 min faDlak, sheel is-sikkeena oo ish-shuwak' oo 'il-malaa9i
6 He must bring all his books with him today
7 Do you (f. sing.) want to speak (the) classical Arabic
   (language)?
8 We cannot go with you (pl.) from Amman to Beirut
9 Bring (pl.) everything with you from the other house
10 Just imagine! He wants to take away all these books!

■ **DIALOGUE: 'The pause that refreshes'**

A   marHaba! mumkin taakhud hal-kutub, min faDlak?
B   HaaDir! haat!
A   shukran! laazim 'artaaH hawn shwayy
B   'ahlan wa sahlan!

Translation

A   Hullo! Could you please take these books?
B   At your service! Let me have them!
A   Thanks! I must rest here for a moment
B   You are welcome!

PROVERB

naam bakkeer, 'oom bakkeer, shoof iS-SiHHa, kayf bitSeer!—
Early to bed, early to rise, makes a man healthy, wealthy and wise!

LESSON SEVEN
VERBS, DEFECTIVE AND DOUBLED

Defective and doubled verbs are grouped together (although in classical Arabic their conjugations differ quite considerably) because in colloquial Arabic their variations from their own basic form are all similar in the past tense. In the non-past, however, they may be regarded as different conjugations.

PAST TENSE

	Defective	*Doubled*
3 m. sing.	masha (*walk*)	dall (*guide*)
2 m. sing.	mash/ayt/	dall/ayt/
3 pl.	mashoo	dalloo

Full conjugations, past tense, are:

Defective verbs (ending in /a/)

	Singular	*Plural*
1 c.	'arayt (*read*)	'arayna
2 m.	'arayt	'araytoo
2 f.	'arayti	'araytoo
3 m.	'ara	'aroo
3 f.	'arat	'aroo

(Those who know classical Arabic will recognize *'ara* as *qara'a*, i.e. a final hamzated verb. In colloquial Arabic the distinction between such and defective verbs disappears.)

Doubled verbs (radicals 2 and 3 the same)

	Singular	*Plural*
1 c.	Dallayt (*remain*)	Dallayna
2 m.	Dallayt	Dallaytoo
2 f.	Dallayti	Dallaytoo
3 m.	Dall	Dalloo
3 f.	Dallat	Dalloo

NON-PAST TENSE

Defective verbs

As opposed to classical Arabic, these verbs in colloquial Arabic tend to have final /a/ or /ee/.

Past	*Non-past*
masha (*walk*)	byimshee
'ara (*read*)	byi'ra
da9a (*invite*)	byid9ee (/-oo/ *in classical Arabic*)

Conjugation rule

Where /-a/ or /-ee/ comes before final /-oo/, /-oo/ dominates.

3 pl. — byimshoo, byi'roo, byid9oo

Exercise

Conjugate these three verbs fully.

Imperative

Non-past	*Imperative*		
	m. sing.	*f. sing.*	*pl.*
byi'ra	'i'ra!	'i'ree!	'i'roo!
byimshee	'imshee!	'imshee!	'imshoo!
byid9ee	'id9ee	'id9ee!	'id9oo!

Doubled verbs

Past-tense *Dall* becomes non-past *byiDall*. But three possibilities exist for the vowel before radical 2.

Past	*Non-past*
Dall (*remain*)	byiDall
madd (*extend*)	byimidd
HaTT (*put*)	byiHuTT

Apart from the above, doubled verbs conjugate with the same prefixes and/or suffixes as *katab byuktub* etc.

Exercise

Conjugate the above three verbs fully.

Imperative

Past	*Non-past*	*Imperative*		
		m. sing.	*f. sing.*	*pl.*
Dall	byiDall	Dall!	Dallee!	Dalloo!
madd	byimidd	midd!	middee!	middoo!
HaTT	byiHuTT	HuTT	HuTTee!	HuTToo!

Participles

On the pattern *HaTT*; *HaaTiT*; *maHTooT*.

DERIVED FORMS

Defective verbs

Past tense

The suffixes change exactly as in defective verbs, Form I.

	II	III	IV	V
3 m. sing.	mashsha	laa'a	'a9Ta	ta9ashsha
	(make walk)	(meet)	(give)	(dine)
1 c.	mashshayt	laa'ayt	'a9Tayt	ta9ashshayt

VI	VII	VIII	X
talaa'a	'inHaka	'ishtara	'istaHla
(meet)	(be said)	(buy)	(find sweet)
(talaa'ayt)	('inHakayt)	'ishtarayt	'istaHlayt

Non-past tense

Two simple rules cover all forms:
1 V, VI and VII have final /-a/
2 All other forms end in /ee/

	II	III	IV	V
Past	mashsha	laa'a	'a9Ta	ta9ashsha
Non-past	byimashshee	byilaa'ee	bya9Tee	byita9ashsha

	VI	VII	VIII	X
	talaaa	'inHaka	'ishtara	'istaHla
	byitalaa'a	'byinHaka	byishtaree	byistaHlee

In addition to the above two rules are added the previous rules for the non-past of simple defective verbs (e.g. /-eeoo/ becomes /-oo).

	V	VIII	X
3 pl.	byita9ashshoo	byishtaroo	byistaHloo

Note Give ('a9Ta) takes two direct objects:

I gave her the book—'a9Tayt-ha il-kitaab
I gave her it—'a9Tayt-ha 'iyyaa(h)

Exercise Conjugate the above Forms II–X.

Derived forms, doubled verbs

Past tense

Form II   Quite normal.
jaddad (renew) takes the suffixes of *katab* (Form I)

Form III   Quite normal.

'aaSaS (punish) takes the suffixes of *katab* (I)

Form IV   Takes the suffixes of Form I *doubled verbs*.

'aSarr (insist) becomes *'aSarrayt* (I insisted)

Form V   Quite normal.

tajaddad (be renewed) takes the same suffixes as *jaddad* (II, renew)

Form VI   Quite normal.

ta'aaSaS (be punished) takes the same ending as *'aaSaS* (III, punish)

Form VII   Takes the same endings as Form I, *doubled* third-person masculine singular.

'in9add (be counted) becomes (1 pl.) *'in9addayna*

Form VIII   Takes the same endings as Form I, *doubled* third-person masculine singular.

'ihtamm (be interested) becomes (1 pl.) *'ihtammayna*

Form IX   This is the only use of Form IX in colloquial Arabic. Doubled verbs Form IX indicate *colours* (and defects in classical Arabic) and conjugate like Form I, doubled.

3 m. sing.	'iHmarr	'iswadd	'iKhDarr
	(red)	(black)	(green)
1 c.	'iHmarrayt	'iswaddayt	'ikhDarrayt

Form X   Behaves like Form I, doubled third-person masculine singular.

ista9add (prepare) becomes (1 pl.) *'ista9addayna*

Non-past

	Past 3 m. sing.	Non-past 3 m. sing.
II	jaddad	byijaddid (*like* 9allam)
III	'aaSaS	byi'aaSiS (*like* kaatab)
IV	'aSarr	byiSirr
V	tajaddad	byitajaddad (*like* ta9allam)
VI	ta'aaSaS	byita'aaSaS (*like* takaatab)
VII	'in9add	byin9add
VIII	'ihtamm	'byihtamm
IX	'iHmarr	byiHmarr
X	ista9add	byista9idd

Note

1 As in hollow verbs, derived forms, Forms II, III, V and VI, behave like verbs such as *katab*.
2 IV and X have the characteristic final vowel /i/, while VII and VIII have characteristic /a/.
3 When suffixes are added to the above, radicals 2 and 3 are never split. For example:

They are interested—byihtammoo

The imperative: come! *ta9aal!*

This comes from the classical Arabic Form VI defective verb:

	m. sing.	f. sing.	pl.
Come!	ta9aal!	ta9aalee!	ta9aaloo!

The prepositions *'ila* (to) and *9ala* (on) + pronouns

	Singular		Plural	
1 c.	'ilee	9alay	'ilaynaa	9alaynaa
2 m.	'ilak	9alayk	'ilaykum/koo	9alaykum/oo
2 f.	'ilik	9alayki	'ilaykum/koo	9alaykum/oo
3 m.	'ilo	9alay(h)	'ilhum	9alayhum
3 f.	'ilha	9alayha	'ilhum	9alayhum

■ VOCABULARY

Verbs

relate, tell (story), speak—Haka, byiHkee
throw—rama, byirmee
let (Let's go!), leave—khalla (II), byikhallee
meet each other—'ilta'a (VIII), byilta'ee; ta'aabal, talaa'a

Nouns/adjectives

city—madeena (*pl.* mudun)
place—maHall (*pl.* -aat), makaan (*pl.* amaakin)
in the morning-—SabaaHan
in the evening—masaa'an
same, self—nafs (+ *noun or pronoun*)
tomorrow—bukra
necessary—Darooree
you don't *have* to go—mush Darooree tarooH
(cf. you must not go—mush laazim tarooH)
life—Hayaa(t)

Particles

thus, so—hayk
(NB such things as that—hayk 'ashyaa)
therefore, and so—li-hayk
inside—juwwa; daakhil
outside—barra

■ EXERCISE

Translate:

1 shoo 'ult 'ilo? maa 'ult 'ilo shee!
2 wayn raayiH? mush raayiH maHall!
3 hayk il Hayaa(t)! yawm 'ilak, yawm 9alayk
4 biddee 'aHuTT hal-kutub fee nafs il-makaan
5 laa, HuTT-hum hawn, 9indee, min faDlak!
6 Let us meet tomorrow at 6.45 in the evening
7 You don't have to go before you see him

8   When you go outside you get sunburned (be red!)
9   After you (f. sing.) see her go to her house
10 Everyone must be interested in his work

■ **DIALOGUE: Being taken for a ride**

A   biddee aroo ila 9ammaan. btaakhud minnee kam?
B   mitl-maa biddak!
A   laa, 'ool lee! 9ashara, miyya, maa ba9rif
B   Tayyib, 'ool khamseen!
A   laa, haada ikteer! btaakhud 9ishreen?
B   laa, mush mumkin, wallaahee!
A   Tayyib, ma9 is-salaama!
B   yallaah! 'iTla9! baakhud minnak khams oo 9ishreen

Translation

A   I want to go to Amman. How much (will you take from me)?
B   Just as you wish!
A   No, tell me! 10 . . . 100: I don't know
B   OK (Let's) say fifty
A   No, that's too much! Will you take twenty?
B   No, by God! Impossible!
A   OK. Goodbye!
B   Come on! Get in! I'll take (from you) twenty-five

PROVERB

ba9d il-ghada tamadda, ba9d il-9asha tamashsha!—Take a rest after lunch, take a walk after dinner

LESSON EIGHT
ASSIMILATED VERBS,
CONJUNCTIONS AND 'FOR'

ASSIMILATED VERBS

initial /w/ mainly; very few initial /yaa/ verbs.

Past tense: initial /w/

Form I: conjugation exactly as for *katab*. Participles quite regular: *waSal* has *waaSil* and *mawSool*.

Exercise

Conjugate *waSal* (arrive); *wa'af* (stand)

Derived forms

Form				
	II	stop someone/something	wa''af	
	III	continue something	waaSal	
	IV	make someone lonely, sad	'awHash	conjugation regular: as for *katab*
	V	stop (intransitive)	tawa''af	
	VI	be continuous	tawaaSal	
	VII	be situated/found (not a classical Arabic verb)	'inwajad	
	VIII	be united	ittaHad	from w-H-d: notice assimilation; otherwise like *katab*
	X	establish a settlement, be a colonizer	'istawTan	conjugation regular

Active and passive participles

Quite regular. For example, Form X: *mustawTin* and *mustawTan*.

58

Exercise

List active and passive participle, for the above derived forms.

Past tense: initial /ya/

Only two (of the very few available) are used in colloquial: one meaning *despair*, the other *wake up*. (It is uncertain if there is a moral there, somewhere.)

Form I   despair: *ya'as*. Conjugation as for *katab*.

Form X   awake: *istay'aZ* from *ya-'-Z*). Conjugation as for *katab*.

A Form V verb is possible: *tayassar*, to be available

Non-past tense: initial /w/

Form I

As opposed to classical Arabic, which drops the initial /w/, colloquial Arabic regards it as a full consonant.

	Past	*Non-past*
arrive	waSal	byooSal
pain	waja9	byooja9
stand	wa'af	byoo'af

Derived forms As for verbs of the *katab* type.

The initial /w/ is maintained in all Forms except VIII, where it becomes *assimilated*.

	Past	*Non-past*
II	wa''af	byiwa''if
III	waaSal	byiwaaSil
IV	'awHash	byooHish
V	tawa''af	byitawa''af
VI	tawaaSal	byitawaaSal
VII	inwajad	byinwajid (*or final* /a/)
VIII	ittaHad	byittaHid
X	'istawTan	byistawTin

Non-past tense: initial /ya/

The rules for initial /w/ apply. In the few verbs with initial /ya/ the /ya/ behaves as a consonant.

	Past	Non-past
despair	ya'as	yay'as
be available	tayassar (V)	yatayassar
awake	istay'aZ	yistay'iZ

Participles of initial /ya/ *verbs*

	Active	Passive
ya'as	yaa'is	may'oos
tayassar	mutayassir	mutayassar
'istay'aZ	mustay'iZ	mustay'aZ

THE SISTERS OF *'ANNA*

The above is the translation of the Arabic term for a group of conjunctions which behave in the same way as the word *'anna* (the conjunction *that*).

	Alone	With pronouns
that	'in (*CA* 'anna)	(3 *m. sing.*) 'inno
because	li-'an (*CA* li-'anna)	(3 *m. sing.*) li-anno
but	(wa) laakin (*CA* walaakinna)	(3 *m. sing.*) (wa) laakinno
since, because, whereas		(3 *m.*) Hays-inno

Examples

1   He went to Amman because his son was there—raaH 'ila 9amman li-'an 'ibno kaan hunaak
2   I know that you arrived here two days ago—ba9rif 'inkum wasalToo la-hawn 'abl yawmayn
3   I wanted to see him but he had gone—kaan biddee 'ashoofo laakinno kaan raaH
4   Because he is a good man I don't want to take any money from him—Hays-'inno rajul Tayyib maa biddee 'aakhud minno fuloos

THE PREPOSITION 'FOR' AND PRONOUNS (*LA +*)

	Singular	*Plural*
1 c.	lee *or* 'ilee	lana *or* 'ilna
2 m.	lak *or* 'ilak	lakum *or* 'ilkum
2 f.	lik *or* 'ilik	lakum *or* 'ilkum
3 m.	lo *or* 'ilo	lahum *or* 'ilhum
3 f.	laha *or* 'ilha	lahum *or* 'ilhum

■ **VOCABULARY**

Verbs

call (out to)—naada (III), byinaadee
clean—naDDaaf (II), byinaDDif
offer (to)—9araD, byi9rad (9ala)
oppose—9aaraD (III), byi9aariD
allow, permit (to) (+ verb in non-past)—samaH, byismaH (la)

Nouns

idea—fikra (*pl.* fikar, 'afkaar)
officer—Daabit (*pl.* DubbaaT)
friend, owner—SaaHib (*pl.* 'aSHaab)
official, employee—muwaZZaf (*pl.* -een)
opportunity, chance—furSa (*pl.* furaS)
past—maaDee
peace—salaam
people (in general)—naas
people (e.g. the French)—sha9b (*pl.* shu9oob)
hand—yad (*f.*; *pl.* aydee)

Note Parts of the body in pairs are feminine (ear, hand etc.).

Particles

certainly, of course—ma9loom
naturally, of course—Tab9an
true, correct—SaHeeH
(*as a question*: Is that so?—SaHeeH?)

■ **EXERCISE**

Translate:

1 shoo fee? yadee btooja9nee
2 9araD 9alayya yinaDDif lee is-sayyaara
3 kull 9aSHaabee 9aaruDoonee 9indmaa 9araDT 9alayhum hal-
   fikra
4 HaDart 'ilal-madrasa li-annhum jaaboo ma9hum 'aSHaabak
5 is-sayyaara tawa''afat fee nuSS il-madeena
6 Do you want to see his new car?
7 There is nothing to be found like it in the whole city
8 Of course not all our friends will arrive at the same time (hour)
9 Will you allow me to stop the car?
10 The officer gave me this book

Make the above singular, plural, feminine, negative, interrogative etc.

■ **DIALOGUE: Car-wash facilities**

A marHaba! bti'dir tnaDDif lee is-sayyaara?
B ma9loom! 'ayya saa9a biddak 'iyyaaha?
A ba9d shee saa9atayn. 9indee shughl fil-madeena
B Haadir! ta9aal ba9d nuSS saa9a btlaa'eeha naDeefa mitl
   sayyaara jadeeda!
A Tayyib! shukran!
B laa shukran 9ala waajib!

Translation

A Hullo! Can you clean this car for me?
B Of course! What time do you want it?
A In about two hours. I have some work in the city.
B At your service. Come back in half an hour and you'll find it like
   a new car.
A Fine! Thanks!
B You're welcome. (lit. 'There is no thanks for a duty!')

PROVERB

laa Hayaata li-man tunaadee (*CA*)—It's like talking to a brick wall
(*lit.* 'there is no life in him to whom you call')

LESSON NINE
RELATIVE PRONOUNS, VERBAL NOUNS AND POSSESSION

THE RELATIVE PRONOUN (who, which, etc.)

This construction in Arabic is simplicity itself, in comparison with English.

The man whom I saw, *the man I saw*, *the man that I saw* are three perfectly acceptable spoken and written usages in English. Furthermore, dialects may say *The man who ('oo) I saw*; *the man what (wot) I saw*, not to mention *the man as I saw* and *the man worr I saw*, etc. All of these are rendered in practically every dialect through the Arabic-speaking world as follows:

ir-rajul 'illee shufto

The complexities of English are not to be found in Arabic. ('This is a thing up with which I will not put.' 'A preposition is something which you should not end a sentence with.')

Rules

1 *'illee* is invariable for all genders and numbers: case does not arise because
2 *'illee* is best regarded as a word linking two co-ordinate sentences (as its name in Arabic grammar implies)
3 When the antecedent is indefinite, *'illee* is omitted.

Examples

He is the man who went to Beirut—huwa ir-rajul *'illee* raaH 'ila bayroot
He is the man whom I saw in Beirut—huwa 'ir-rajul *'illee* shufto fee bayroot.
They are the men in whose car I went to Beirut—hum 'ir- rijaal *'illee* ruHt 'ila bayroot fee sayyaarat-hum
She is the woman in whose sister's car I went to Beirut—hiyya 'il-mara *illee* ruHt 'ila bayroot fee sayyaarat 'ukht-ha

There's a girl here who wants to speak to you—fee bint hawn bidd-ha tiHkee ma9ak

From these examples it can be seen that when translating from English one first makes two sentences which contain the same meaning. These sentences are translated and then linked with *'illee* (omitted when the antecedent is indefinite).

This is the explanation for the slightly odd-looking 'the man (whom) I saw *him*'.

THE VERBAL NOUN

This is roughly the equivalent of the 'infinitive' (to write, to see etc.), but also equates with the so-called gerund (e.g. 'seeing is believing').

Arabic would use the verbal noun in the above cases.

Examples

Writing Arabic is easy—kitaabat 'il-lugha 'il-9arabiyya sahla
He likes reading and writing—byiHibb 'il-'iraya oo il-kitaaba

(**Note** The verbal noun is usually definite.)

Uses of the verbal noun

Arabic uses the verbal noun where English frequently uses some other construction. An example is airport flight announcements. Where English says 'Would passengers please proceed . . .' etc. Arabic says 'The proceeding of the passengers is requested. . . .'

Examples

1   *Adverbially*

He hit him hard—Darabo *Darab* (lit. ..ᴇ *hit him a hitting*')

In this usage the verbal noun may take an adjective, for example:

He hit him repeatedly (a continuous hitting)—Darabo Darab mutawaa Sil

2 *In place of clauses*

After Muhammad arrived—ba9ad *wuSool* muHammad

3 *As the infinitive*

He likes to visit the Arabic countries—byiHibb *zeeaarat* il-bilaad
  'il-9arabiyya

4 *As the gerund*

He likes travelling—byiHibb is-safar

5 *To render 'as . . . as' etc.* Arabic does not have the equivalent
small words of German, French and English (*so . . . wie*; *aussi . . .
que*; as . . . as), but among ways of rendering such constructions is
the use of the verbal noun.

He is as interested in English as he is in Arabic—byihtamm bil-
  lugha il-inkleeziyya *ihtimaamo* bil-lugha il-9arabiyya

6 *To render a variety of clauses*

(a) because the students are not here—bisabab *9adam* (*lack*)
     wujood iT-Tulaab (*lit.* 'the lack of the presence of . . .')
(b) because the students may attend—bisabab *'imkaaniyyat
     HuDoor* iT-Tullaab ('because of the possibility of the students'
     attendance')

7 *In formal Arabic:* for example *notices* or *announcements* which
may be broadcast and will therefore be part of the student's contact
with spoken Arabic.

no smoking—mamnoo9 (*forbidden*) *it-tadkheen*
no parking—mamnoo9 (*forbidden*) *il-wu'oof*
please (come forward)—*'ar-rajaa* (*both parts are v.ns*) *'al-HuDoor*

8 *In idioms*

absolutely beautiful—fee muntaha *al-jamaal*

(**Note** 3 and 4 above are very common in colloquial Arabic; 1, 2, 5,
6, 7 and 8 are used in a slightly elevated form of colloquial Arabic,
or, indeed, in standard written Arabic.)

Forms of the verbal noun

Wright's *Arabic Grammar* lists forty-four forms possible for the verbal noun (apart from the derived forms which have standard patterns for each form). It is not necessary to *memorize* these forms, but the student will need to memorize the form(s) occurring for each particular verb. (These are given in the vocabulary lists at the end of the book.) Some common forms are:

		Past	*Verbal noun*
1	understand	fahim	fahm
2	be glad	fariH	faraH
3	sit	jalas	juloos

The forms for *derived-form verbal nouns* are as follows:

II	teach	9allam	ta9leem
III	consult	shaawar	mushaawara
IV	throw out	'akhraj	'ikhraaj
V	learn	ta9allam	ta9allum
VI	write to one another	takaatab	takaatub
VII	be written	'inkatab	'inkitaab
VIII	assemble	'ijtama9	'ijtimaa9
IX	be red (become red)	'iHmarr	'iHmiraar
X	employ, use	'ista9mal	isti9maal

POSSESSION

Levantine Arabic has another formula for indicating possession, in addition to the *construct* (Lesson one) and *9ind* (Lesson two). This is the word *taba9* (cf. classical Arabic *taabi9*, meaning 'subordinate to, belonging to'). *taba9* has a variety of uses

1 his book—'il-kitaab taba9o
2 the book of the boy—'il-kitaab taba9 il-walad
3 The book belongs to the boy—'il-kitaab taba9 il-walad

(There is a difference in intonation between the above: 3 is an example of an equational sentence; hence the lack of a verb.)

Whose is this book?—hal-kitaab taba9 meen? (*Also* la-meen hal-kitaab?)

In some Levantine dialects *taba9* has a feminine, *taba9a*, and a plural, *taba9een*. For example:

his boys—'il-'awlaad taba9eeno

■ **VOCABULARY**

Verbs

help—saa9ad
work—'ishtaghal, byishtaghil
laugh (at)—DaHak, byiDHak (9ala)
wash—ghassal, byighassil
try—jarrab, byijarrib
think—'iftakar, byiftikir

Nouns/adjectives

early—bakkeer
north—shimaal
south—janoob
east—shar'
west—gharb
education—tarbeea
Egypt—maSir (*f.*), miSr
private—khuSooSee (*f.* -iyya)
programme—barnaamaj (*pl.* baraamij)

Particles

during—'asnaa
while—baynamaa
pardon: I beg your pardon (reply to thanks)—il-9afoo *or* 9afwan
now—halla
not yet (gone)—maa (raaH) ba9d, lissa maa (raaH)
some *other* book—ghayr kitaab
some one *other* than they—ghayrhum
some *other* time—ghayr marra

■ **EXERCISE**

Translate:

1   has-sayyaara taba9 meen?
2   il-maktoob 'illee Hattayto 9alaT-Taawila mush hawn halla
3   'il-bint illee ta9arrafna 9alayha 'umrha 9ashar sanawaat
4   kullhum dakhaloo il-ghurfa 'illee kunna mujtami9een feeha
5   sami9na 'inno raayiH 'ila 9ammaan fis-sayyaara 'illee ishtaraaha
    fee bayroot
6   Do you know who is the man they were laughing at?
7   Whose are the books you brought with you?
8   Before you wash your hands (*eedayk*) leave your books here.
9   Don't laugh at him, he's trying
10 Who was that lady I saw you with?

*Make the above sentences negative, plural, interrogative etc., where
feasible.*

■ **DIALOGUE: Brief encounter**

A   ta9aal! biddee 9arrifak 9ala 'aSHaabee!
B   shukran! meen iD-DaabiT 'illee waa'if ma9 'aHmad?
A   haada 'abdul waaHid, musaa9id is-safeer
B   biftikir, shufto 'abl shahr 'asnaa 'iz-zeeaara 'illee 9amilnaaha 'ila
    lundun
A   SaHeeH! 'ana oo iyyaah kunna fee lundun fee nafs 'il-wa't

Translation

A   Come (on)! I want to introduce you to my friends
B   Thanks! . . . Who's the officer standing with Ahmad?
A   That's Abdul-Wahid, the Ambassador's assistant (aide)
B   I think I saw him a month ago during the visit we made to
    London
A   That's right! He and I were in London at the same time

PROVERB

btiHkee(h) fish-shar' byijaawibak fil-gharb—He is unpredictable
(and probably not very bright) (lit. 'You speak to him in the east, he
replies in the west')

LESSON TEN
MORE VERBS, VERBAL PHRASES
AND WHENEVER/WHOEVER

QUADRILITERAL VERBS

These verbs are unusual only in the sense that they are based on words not falling into the tri-consonantal pattern. Their conjugation, however, is quite consistent. A common type is the verb *tarjam*, meaning 'translate' (the origin of the old-fashioned word for an Oriental translator *dragoman*, from *tarjumaan*).

Past	Non-past	Participles		Verbal noun
Form I				
tarjam	byitarjim	mutarjim	mutarjam	tarjama
Form II				
tafarnaj (behave like a *faranjee*, i.e. ape foreigners)	byitafarnaj	mutafarnij	mutafarnaj	tafarnuj
ta'a'lam (become acclimatized)	byita'a'lam	muta'a'lim	muta'a'lam	ta'a'lum

TO COME

The nearest thing to an irregular verb in colloquial Arabic. The suffixes are consistent but the rest is unstable.

	Past	Non-past	Active participle
3 m. sing.	'aja	byeejee	jaa'ee

(Remember from Lesson seven the odd imperative *come!*—ta9aal.)

Past-tense conjugation

	Singular	Plural
1 c.	jeet	jeena
2 m.	jeet	jeetoo

	Singular	Plural
2 f.	jeetee	jeetoo
3 m.	'aja	'ajoo
3 f.	'ajat	'ajoo

Clearly the verb is unsure if it is a hollow one or not.

Non-past

	Singular	Plural
1 c.	bajee	mneejee
2 m.	bteejee	bteejoo
2 f.	bteejee	bteejoo
3 m.	byeejee	byeejoo
3 f.	bteejee	byeejoo

HAAL CLAUSES

So called from the classical Arabic term for a class of adverbial clauses.

I learned the language *when I was small*—ta9allamt 'il-lugha *oo 'ana 'iSgheer (or iZgheer)*

I saw him *as I was coming to school*—shufto oo 'ana jaayee lil-madrasa

compare I saw him (*as he was*) coming—shufto jaayee

Note the extension of this:

I saw *him writing*—shufto 9am byuktub

WHENEVER/WHOEVER ETC.

anything whatever—shoo maa kaan
anytime at all—aya wa't (*or classical Arabic* waqtin) kaan
whatever he does—mahmaa bya9mal
no matter how tired he is—mahmaa byikoon ta9baan
anytime (whenever) you like—wa't maa btreed
as much as you like—'add maa btreed
whoever you wish—meen maa btreed
as soon as—Haalmaa

THE VERB *SAAR* **('become')**

Note the idiomatic uses of *Saar*:

1   They began to write—Saaroo yuktuboo (+ *non-past; both verbs conjugate, non-past with no* b/m *prefix*)

2   (a) They have been here two months—Saar lahum shahrayn hawn

(b) We have been waiting two hours—Saar 'il-na saa9atayn nantaZir hawn

(i.e. *Sar* 3 m. sing. impersonal, unchanging: the pronouns following *'ila* or *la* change. Any verb following is non-past. Cf. French *'j'attends depuis 2 heures'*)

3   (a) They have *already* gone—Saaroo raayiHeen

(b) We had already gone—kunna Sirna raayiHeen

■   **VOCABULARY**

Verbs

spend a summer holiday—Sayyaf, byiSayyif
rain—shattat (id-dunya), bitshattee
prefer . . . to . . .—faDDal . . . 9ala . . ., byifaDDil
come near, move (intransitive, either to or from the speaker)—
    'arrab, byi'arrib

Nouns/adjectives

mistake—ghalaT (*pl.* ghalTaat)
wrong number—numra ghalaT
summer—Sayf
winter—shitaa
spring—rabee9
autumn—khareef
in a hurry, 'express'—musta9jal
peasant—fallaaH (*pl.* -een)
difficult—Sa9b
free (i.e. no work)—faaDee (*pl.* -een)

Particles

without—bidoon, bilaa
doubtless—bi-laa shakk, bidoon shakk
Forget it! (lit. 'Without it!')—bi-laa-haa!

■ **EXERCISE**

Translate:

1 Haayaat il-fallaaHeen 'ikteer Sa9ba fish-shitaa
2 Wayn bitSayyif, fish-shaam aw fee 9ammaan?
3 bufaDDil 'annak teejee wa't maa btkoon faaDee
4 'il 'ajaanib byiHibboo yeejoo 'ilal-bilaad fish-shitaa li-'ann
   bilaad-hum feeha bard
5 shufto jaayee bass ma kaan 9indee wa't 'uwa''if is-sayyaara
6 It was raining as I came from the city
7 Does it rain a great deal in Lebanon in the spring?
8 Please could you give me Mr Ahmad! Wrong number!
9 I will come to the office as soon as I see him
10 Do you want to come in the new car we have bought, my
   friends and I?

■ **DIALOGUE: Translator wanted**

A 'ool lee bta9rif titarjim inkleezee 9arabee?
B shway, bass, shoo, 9indak shee biddak titarjimo?
A laa, bass baHibb 'ata9arraf 9ala waaHid bya9rif il-lughatayn
   kwayyis.
B Tayyib, ba'ool lak shoo. 9indee Sadee' 'almaanee bya9rif
   inkleezee kwayyis oo bya9rif 9arabee 'aHsan minnee oo
   minnak!
A 'a9Teenee ismo, 9indak ra'm talfoono?
B na9am, 9indee iyyaah hawn

Translation

A Tell me, can you translate English/Arabic?
B Only a little. What('s the matter)? Have you something you
   want to translate?

A   No, but I'd like to get to know someone who knows both languages well.
B   OK, I tell you what. I have a German friend who knows English well and knows Arabic better than you and I do.
A   Give me his name. Do you have his phone number?
B   Yes, I have it here.

PROVERB

'a9Tee khubzak lil-khabbaaz wa law 'akal nuSSo—Give your bread to the baker, even if he eats half of it (i.e. always consult an expert or professional)

LESSON ELEVEN
CONDITIONAL SENTENCES

CONDITIONAL SENTENCES ('If . . .')

1   The rules for **classical** Arabic 'if' sentences are very elaborate, but the colloquial rules are much simpler.

2   **Real or 'probable' conditional sentences**
Arabic uses *'iza* for 'if' in sentences such as:

If you see him tell him I'm here—iza btshoofo 'ool lo 'ana hawn

3   **Unreal or 'impossible' conditional sentences**
law is used:

if I had a million dollars—law kaan 9indee milyoon doolaar

4   The rules for **sequence of tenses** are much less elaborate than in classical Arabic.

If they had gone that way down to Beirut they would be there by now—law kaanoo nazaloo ila bayroot min hunaak kaanoo waSaloo (halla').

5   A classical word for 'if' ('*in*) is used in some formal expressions. The most famous is:

If God wills—in shaa' 'allaa(h) (*or* 'inshalla(h))

Note   (a) The classical *in* is used:
(b) the classical sequence of tenses is used;
(c) '*allaah* is the only word in all Arabic with such a dark /*l*/ sound (velarization). Other Levantine formulae include
(d) If God wills—in 'allaa(h) raad (*or* 'araad)

6   NB   unless I'm mistaken—'in lam akun ghalTaan

■ **VOCABULARY**

Verbs

finish—khallaS, byikhalliS
destroy—kharrab, byikharrib
specialize (in)—takhaSSaS (fee)
believe—Sadda', byiSaddi'

Nouns/adjectives

broken down, worn out, out of order—kharbaan
national, patriotic—waTanee
hair—sha9r (*pl.* -aat)
poetry—shi9r
poet—shaa9ir
journalism—SaHaafa
hotel—fundu' (*pl.* fanaadi')

Particles

for, for the sake of (prep.)—min shaan
in order to, that (conjunction)—Hatta
approximately—ta'reeban
about (subject)—9an
that is to say (lit. 'it means')—ya9nee

■ EXERCISE

Translate:

1 Saddi'nee! haada 'aHsan kitaab bil'inkleezee 9an ish-shi9r il-9
  arabee
2 'ool lee, 'ayya saa9a bitkhalliS shughlak?
3 'iza btrooH ('ila) 9ammaan bitlaa'ee fanaadi' jadeeda ikteer
4 law kunna hawn 'abl sanatayn maa shufna wa-laa madrasa.
  abadan
5 'iza bitlaa'ee kitaab kwayyis bil-9arabee 9an 'ish-shi9r 'il-
  faransaawee jeeb lee 'iyyaah
6 He is coming from Damascus so that he can study journalism in
  the university
7 Did you know that my friend is a specialist in education
  programmes?
8 Would you like anything else?
9 If you want to be introduced to the man you saw here, come to
  my house tomorrow at 9.00 a.m.
10 If I had worked with him I would have become a millionaire
*Make the above sentences plural, feminine, interrogative, etc. where
feasible.*

■ DIALOGUE: Of Arabic poetry

A 'ool lee, shoo raayak? meen 'aHsan shaa9ir 9arabee?
B wallaah, haada su'aal Saa9b ikteer. shaa9ir lubnaanee, ya9nee?
A laa, mush biD-Daroora. 'aSdee, min ayya bilaad 9arabiyya
B Tayyib, fee miSr 9indak 'aHmad shaw'ee, maa fee ghayro
  byisammoo(h) 'ameer ish-shu9araa
A 'aHmad shaw'ee, ba9do Tayyib?
B laa, maat sanat 'alf oo tisa9 miyya oo 'itnayn oo talaateen

Translation

A Tell me, what do you think (what is your opinion)? Who is the
  best Arab poet?
B (By God) that's a very difficult question. A Lebanese poet, do
  you mean ('. . . it means?').

A   Not necessarily. I mean, a poet from any Arab country
B   OK. In Egypt you have Ahmad Shawqi. There's no other (to
    compare). They call him the Prince of Poets
A   Is Ahmad Shawqi still alive?
B   No, he died in 1932

PROVERB

khayrul-kalaami maa qalla wa dall (*classical Arabic, but used widely
in colloquial*)—The best speech is short and to the point ('what is
little and shows the way')

LESSON TWELVE
IDIOMS

The vernacular of the Levant is rich in idioms, as is the vernacular of
any society where speech is prized as an art-form. ('Wisdom alighted
on three things, the brain of the Franks, the hand of the Chinese and
the tongue of the Arabs.') Poetry recitals, songs, Koran recitations,
story-telling, poetry composition, word-games, speech-making, *zajl*
competitions,* are all examples of Arabic language activity which
are still highly prized.

The Levant is no exception among Arabic societies. Before the
Lebanese civil war a *bon mot* at a public *zajl* competition would
often be greeted by enthusiastic small-arms fire. But, apart from
formal activities such as the above, Arabic everyday speech is vivid
and idiomatic. Levantine Arabic is especially rich and varied, as its
geographical area includes coastal plain and mountain, desert and
plateau, villages, rural settlements and metropolitan areas, while the
communities range from trilingual western-orientated city dwellers
to monolingual Bedu; from Druze 'initiates' to Muslim peasants;
and from Imams to Maronite patriarchs and cultivators, not to mention Armenians, Greek Orthodox, Chaldean Catholics, Nestorians,

*Extempore competitions in rhyming colloquial poetry on themes set as
debating topics between rival teams.

Roman Catholics and even Aramaic-speaking communities. Given such variety it is not surprising that there is a wide range of idiom (mariners and mountaineers, peasants and traders, Christian and Muslim, etc.). The approximately 200 idioms which follow are a modest offering from a wealth of possible items.

The arrangement is alphabetical Arabic–English and English–Arabic, taking the initial letter of the main word in the idiom.

'alif

God forbid! (lit. 'I seek a refuge in God from the Devil!')	'a 9oozu billaah min ash-shayTaan 'ar-rajeem!
two-faced (lit. 'father of two tongues')	'aboo lisaanayn

NB
1 For sure! — 'abadan!
2 with neg. = not at all
   a nice chap — aadamee

baa'

No question!	maa feesh baHs!
not so hot, not too good	mush wa-laa budd
Get out!	barra!
That's quite enough!	bass!

taa'

Fantastic!	tuHfa! (*Leb.*)
Just a mo!	takki iZgheera! (*Leb.*)
worn out	ta9baan
They overdid it	takhkhanoo-ha

thaa'

Holy Trinity	ath-thaalooth al-mu'addas
three-quarters	talaat 'arbaa9
twenty minutes	tult saa9a (*one-third of an hour*)

jeem

I'm serious. No joking!	9am baHkee jadd!
Much obliged!	shukran jazeelan!

| The whole thing is . . . (what it all amounts to is . . .) | jull maa fil-'amr |
| He went crazy | jann junoono |

Haa

next to	Hadd
a crafty one	Harboo' (*Leb.*)
Shame on you!	Haraam 9alayk!
He has the luck of the devil (His luck splits rocks!)	HaZZo byifla' il-Hajr

khaa'

sells like hot cakes (bread)	byinbaa9 mitl il-khubz
senile	kharfaan
amiable	khafeef id-damm
Stay here!	khalleek hawn!

dal

Work it out for yourself (*Débrouillez-vous!*)	dabbir Haalak!
please!	dakhlak
simple, nice chap, unpretentious	darweesh
straight ahead (also, honest)	dughree

dhaal(z)

the same thing	ish-shee zaato
'gormless', stupid	bi-laa zaw'
You are really too kind!	kullak zaw' oo LuTf
in X's debt	fee zimmat fulaan

raa'

straight on/ahead/away	ra'san
You have to pay for good value	ir-rakheeS ghaalee
They made fun of us	rakkaboo 9alaynaa
Get a move on!	rawwij! (*Leb.*)

zay

| 'old chap' | yaa zalamee (*Jor.*) |
| a long time ago | min zamaan |

Remove it to one side	zeeHo!
Add to that, that . . .	zid 9ala haada, inno . . .

seen

Praise be! (Muslims only!)	subHaan il-mughayyir!
had already gone	saba' oo raaH
indisposed, ill	saakhin shwayy
It just happened that . . .	saa'abat inno . . . (*Leb.*)

sheen

(Said to avoid evil)	min ghayr sharr
What else can we do?	shoo biddna na9mal?
What's up? What's wrong (with you)?	shoo bik?
Why, of course!	shoo, la-kaan! (*Leb.*)
I want nothing to do with this affair	shoo biddee fee hash-shaghla? (*Leb.*)
Er . . . what I mean is . . .	shoo biddee 'a'ool lak?
What's new?	shoo fee, maa fee? (*Leb.*)
What chaos!	shoo hal-fawDa!
No! you can't mean that!	shoo hal-Hakee!
No! you can't mean that!	shoo 9am btiHkee?
What a bore!	shoo mut9ib!
What an agreeable fellow!	shoo laTeef!

Saad

Patience is beautiful/good	iS-Sabr jameel/Tayyib
moody	SaaHib 'aTwaar
fortunate coincidence	Sudfa khayr min mee9aad
in the direction of . . .	Sawb (*Leb.*) . . .

Daad

Chaos! (The bath-house bowl is missing)	iT-Taasa Dayy9a
Put the light on (for us)!	Dawweel-naa!
I have fixed things!	ZabbaTt-haa!
the Arabic language	lughat-iD-Daad

Taa'

spitting image	Taba' il-'aSl
first-rate	min iT-Tiraaz il-awwal
senseless (talk)	bi-laa Ta9m
gossip	Ta'' Hanak

Zaa'

It seems that . . .	iZ-Zaahir 'inno . . .
He's just gone out	halla' Zahar (*Leb.*)
by heart	9an Zahr 'alb
behind his back	waraa Zahro

9ayn

That doesn't prove a thing	mush 9ibra
a traffic jam	9aj'at sayr (*Leb.*)
in plain language	bil-9arabee il-mushabraH
Raise your voice! Speak up a little!	9allee Sawtak!

ghayn

usually	ghaaliban (maa)
something's afoot	fee shee 9am byighlee
closed his eyes	ghammaD 9aynay(h)
it slipped my mind	ghaab 9an baalee

faa'

Switch on (the radio) to the BBC	iftaH 9a-lundun!
all at one go	fard marra (*Leb.*)
from one piece (e.g. of wood)	fard sha'fa
each (e.g. L. 10 each)	fi'at

qof

common factor (often, 'unifying principle')	qaasim mushtarak

kaaf

(at the) bottom of the village	fee ka9b iD-Day9a (*Leb.*)
nonsense	kalaam faarigh

laam

same old story	latt oo 9ajn
Just a moment!	laHZa iZgheera!

meem

Not bad	mush baTTaal
No! it can't be! (astonishment)	mush ma9'ool!

noon

Just a drop!	nitfa 'iZgheera! (*Leb.*)
(a) boring (person)	naashif

haa'

Give (me)! Bring (me)!	haat!
Let's see (it)	haat tanshoof!
Hullo!	yaa hala!

waw

Not at all! That's the least we could do (for you)!	wa law! waajibna!
Lower your voice!	waTTee Sawtak!
Please (do something for me)! *or* I assure you/believe me!	wa-Hyaatak!
Look out! Mind your back!	'oo9aa!

yaa'

I wonder (if) . . .	yaa turaa . . .
Oh! Lord! (Said when beginning work)	yaa rabb!
Oh! God! (Expression of astonishment)	yaa salaam!

A

all day long	Tool in-nahaar
all right (*ça va*)	maashil-Haal
Anyone there?	fee Hada hunaak?
as much as you like	'add maa btreed

B

back to front	bil-ma'loob
bad language	kalaam bazee'
bear: I can't bear him	mush'aadir ataHammalo
beg: I beg pardon of God	'astaghfir 'allaah!

C

changed his mind	ghayyar fikro
Cheers! (e.g. with a drink)	SaHtayn!
circle: vicious circle	Hal'a mufragha
close friend	Sadee' Hameem

D

dark: it became dark	9atamat id-dunya
death: sick to death; fed up	zah'aan
deep end: go off the deep end	Taar 9a'lo
devil: Poor devil!	miskeen!

E

each other (e.g. on top of each other)	faw' ba9D
easy in mind	murtaaH il-baal
either . . . or . . .	yaa . . . yaa . . .
equals (e.g. 2 + 2 = 4)	byisaawee

F

face: lose face	fa'ad mayy wujho
fall in love with . . .	wa'a9 fee Hubb . . .
fall out (quarrel)	takhaana'oo
feeling: Are you feeling all right?	Haasis bi-shee?

G

give and take	'akhad oo radd
go out of one's mind	Taar 9a'lo
good-for-nothing	mush naafi9
grounds: on the grounds that . . .	9ala 'asaas inno

H

had: You had better go	'aHsan tarooH
hand-in-hand	maasikeen eed ba9D
head over heels	ra'san 9ala 9aqab
here is/are	hayy (+ *pronouns*)
(Here they are!	hayy iyyaahum!)

I

ill: It's an ill wind (etc.)	maSaa'ib qawm 9ind qawm fawaa'id (Al-Mutanabbi)
in: He's not in	mush mawjood
inside out	bil-ma'loob
It's . . . speaking (e.g. phone)	'ana . . .

J

job: It's a good job it wasn't
     worse
	mleeH innha maa kaanat
	      'a9Zam

joking: I'm not joking	mush 9am bamzaH
just: I've just come	ba9dnee jaa'ee
Just so! Exactly!	biZ-ZabT!

K

Keep quiet!	uskut!
kidding: No kidding!	laa, SaHeeH! 9am baHkee jadd!
Kindly (e.g close the door)!	luTfan . . .
know: as far as I know	9ala 9ilmee

L

labour: hard labour	'a9maal shaa''a
land: by land	bil-barr
last: At last!	oo 'akheeran!
late: the late (e.g. king)	'il-marHoom . . .

M

makes no difference to me	maa btifri' ma9ee
means: By no means!	laa, abadan!
middle-aged	fee mutawassiT il-9umr
mind: set his mind on	HaaTiT bi-fikro

N

neck: He got it in the neck	Hara'oo lo bayto
net weight	il-wazn iS-Saafee
Never mind	maa 9alaysh
now: from now on	min halla oo Taali9

O

obliged: Much obliged	mamnoonak
odd: on odd days	kull yawm taanee
Once upon a time . . .	fee yawm min al-ayyaam . . .
owe: I owe you a lira	9alay lak leera

P

pack of lies	kizb fee kizb
pair of shoes	jawz kandara
Pardon me!	il-9afoo!
particular (reason)	(sabab) mu9ayyan

Q

queer (sex)	shaazz
question: It's a question of . . .	il-mas'ala mas'alat . . .
quick-witted	saree9 il-khaaTir
Quite right! Quite so!	tamaaman! biZ-Zabt!

R

rather: or rather . . .	'aw bil-'aHraa . . .
read aloud	'araa bi-Sawt 9aalee
reason: by reason of his work	bi-Hukm shughlo
return: in return for . . .	mu 'aabil . . .

S

saying: as the saying goes	mitl maa byi'ooloo
Search me! (How do I know?)	shoo ba9arrifnee?
still: He's still here	ba9do hawn
Stop!	wa' 'if!

T

Take my word for it!	'isma9 minnee!
taste: not to my taste	mush 9ala zaw'ee
that big/so big (demonstration)	hal 'add

too big	kabeer ikteer; 'akbar min il-laazim

U

under: in under one hour	fee 'a'all min saa9a
up to now	li-ghaayat halla
use: It's no use	maa fee faa'ida
utmost: Do your utmost	i9mal il-mustaHeel

V

very: the very same day	fee nafs ilyawm
view: in view of the circumstances	naZaran liZ-Zuroof
virtue: by virtue of . . .	bi-faDl . . .
visits: They don't exchange visits	maa byizooroo oo maa byinzaaroo

W

Wait a minute!	'istanna shwayy!
wants: He wants for nothing	maa byun'uSo shee
washed up the dishes	ghassalat il 'aTbaa'
whatsit, er . . . you know what I mean	ool ma9ee!

X

X: Mr X	'il-'ustaaz fulaan
X-rays	'ash9iat-iks

Y

Year: Happy New Year (or any annual feast)	kull 9aam oo int bi-khayr
Yes, indeed!	'ay, na9am!
yet: He's not come yet	maa 'ajaa ba9d
yet again	kamaan marra
Yours sincerely	'il-mukhliS

Z

zero hour	saa9at iS-Sifr

LESSON THIRTEEN
TERMS OF ADDRESS AND
REFERENCE

English is poverty-stricken by comparison with Arabic in terms of address and reference. In the Levant one can ring the changes in everyday communication on a great range of titles for people (coupled with a vocative 'O . . . !') depending on whether they are young, old, male or female, venerable, known or unknown, superior or inferior in station, single or in a group, and even according to religious denomination: a priest has a different title from a *mufti*, a Druze elder from a young Druze in modern dress. The terms which follow are a mere selection of those it is possible to hear in the Levant on a typical day between town and village, between home and *souq*, school and office.

Words on a page cannot describe fully the background to the terms given. Only experience can tell the foreigner how to use the terms freely. A start may be made on those expressions which are almost entirely unambiguous, being addressed to people whose status is known, and being, in most cases, meant literally. (*yaa*, the vocative, is invariable and has none of the quaint old fashioned sound of 'O . . .' in English. Exclamation marks and 'O . . .' are omitted in the translation into English.)

ADDRESS
Group A Literal and/or unambiguous terms

Arabic		Meaning	Used to*
1	yaa muHtaram	Respected one	A priest
2	yaa Hakeem	Wise one	A doctor
3	yaa jaar	Neighbour	A neighbour
4	yaa shaaweesh	Sergeant	A sergeant (or lesser rank for purposes of ingratiation)

*But not exclusively, in any particular example below

Arabic	Meaning	Used to*
5 yaa 'ustaaz	Professor	Someone of standing, usually a brain worker (teacher, well-dressed stranger etc.)
6 yaa mu9allim	Teacher	A craftsman: carpenter, mechanic etc.
7 yaa sitt(na)	Lady	A married woman, usually older than the speaker
8 yaa 'aanisa	Miss	A young lady
9 yaa mukhtar	*Mukhtar*	A *mukhtar* or village headman (lit. 'chosen one')
10 yaa walad	Boy	A young boy (possibly to a waiter, but caution is enjoined. Try 6 above)
11 yaa shaykh	Shaikh or elder	An elder, not necessarily a religious man (also a friendly term used to an equal or contemporary)

Group B   Terms used to a group

12 yaa jamaa9a	Group	A group (may be used to call them to order)
13 yaa shabaab	Youths	A group of youngish men (always well-received)

*But not exclusively, in any particular example below

Arabic		*Meaning*	*Used to**
14	yaa zawaat	Excellent ones	A group of un-knowns (flattering, rather old-fashioned)
15	yaa 9aalam	World	See 16
16	yaa naas	People	15 and 16 often together as an indignant protest
17	'ayyuhaa-l-Hafl al-kareem	Noble gathering	Formal address to an audience

Now for a group of terms using words which have a specific kinship meaning, but which are used widely to address a stranger without offence.

Group C   Kinship terms used to strangers

18	yaa 9amm	Paternal uncle	An older man, usually
19	yaa khaal	Maternal uncle	As 18
20	yaa 'ukhtee	My sister	A respectable lady of roughly the same age

Related to group C are a number of terms which, especially in Lebanese Arabic, are used to entirely the wrong person! A grandchild may be addressed as 'Grandfather'!

Group D   Kinship terms used 'wrongly'

21	yaa jiddo	His grandfather	Very affectionate: to a grandchild
22	yaa bayyee	My father	To a son!
23	yaa 9ammo	His uncle	To a nephew, but also to a stranger in friendly fashion
24	yaa khaalo	As 23	As 23

*But not exclusively, in any particular example below

Group E is another group where the term is not necessarily to be understood literally.

Group E   Flattery

Arabic	*Meaning*	*Used to**
25 yaa 9arees	Bridegroom	Good-looking (or not!) young stranger
26 yaa shabb	Young man	As 25
27 yaa bay	Bey (Ottoman title)	Possibly ingratiating, but can be used jokingly
28 yaa baasha	Pasha (Ottoman title)	As 27
29 yaa mawlaanaa	Our Lord(!)	As 27
30 yaa seedee	Sir	As 27 (very common in Damascus)

The next group is possibly the most ambiguous, and is the one which calls for the most caution: a little knowledge is a dangerous thing. However, to plunge in, the main characteristic of this group is excessive flattery.

Group F   Excessive flattery

Nos 31–4 can be used to strangers, especially an official dealing with the public.

31 yaa rooHee	My spirit	
32 yaa 9aynee	My eye	
33 yaa Habeebee	My dear/darling	
34 yaa 'albee	My heart	
35 yaa shaaTir	Clever one	To a young boy
36 yaa kwayyis	Excellent one	As 35, but many other uses
37 yaa Tayyib	Good one	As 36
38 yaa sitt il-kull	Mistress (i.e. lady) of all	To (older?) women; slightly bantering

*But not exclusively, in any particular example below

Group G   Grand titles, but of obligatory usage

Arabic	Meaning	Used to*
39 yaa HaDrat . . .	Your Honour	Depends on addressee; e.g. no. 40:
40 yaa HaDrat il-'un-Sul	Your Honour the Consul	(Many other combinations in the above forty styles of address)
41 yaa dawlat arra'ees	Dawla ('state' in political science)	A Prime Minister
42 yaa ma9aaleekum	'Votre Excellence'	A minister in government (or ex-)
43 yaa sa9aadat is-safeer	His Excellency the Ambassador	An ambassador
44 yaa samaaHat il-muftee	Eminence	A mufti
45 yaa fakhaamat ar-ra'ees	Excellency	A President of the Republic
46 yaa ghibTat il-baTriark	Beatitude	A cardinal of the Church

And finally a group of terms used which are addressing God, if translated literally, but which have other uses. All are taken from the ninety-nine 'Most Beautiful Names of God'.

Group H   Calling on the Almighty

47 yaa salaam!	Peace	To express astonishment
48 yaa laTeef!	Kindly One	As 47
49 yaa saatir!	Protector	To ward off trouble, especially after mention thereof

*But not exclusively, in any particular example below

Arabic	*Meaning*	*Used to**
50 yaa allaah!	Allah	Many uses; often, e.g. 'how could anyone be so brazen as to do/say a thing like that!'

The above categories are by no means exhaustive, and each category has many additional terms. Furthermore each term could be described at greater length: for example *yaa 9azeezee, yaa Habeebee* ('my dear, my darling') could be used in exasperation or remonstrance. And so on. . . . However, the above are an indispensable minimum which the student should recognize and begin to use.

REFERENCE

Very often such terms are the obverse of terms of reference. For example, when referring to some distinguished person one would say *HaDirto*, whereas one would address him as *HaDirtak* (His/ Your Honour). A Muslim religious dignitary would be referred to as *samaaHto*.

Three terms should be noted which overlap address and reference. In asking, 'What is your name?', one may say:

1 shoo'ism il-'akh?   What is the name of the brother?
2 shoo'ism il-kareem?   What is the name of the noble one?
3 shoo'ism il-9azeez?   What is the name of the dear one?

Such formulae could be used for many questions: for example 'Where are you from?', 'Is this yours?' and so on.

ADDRESS AND REFERENCE IN RELIGIOUS TERMS

Scores of terms may be used to address a stranger in Islamic terms: *yaa 9abdo!* ('O, His slave!') is an example. Indeed, in some dialects any male stranger may be acceptably addressed as *yaa muHammad!*

*But not exclusively, in any particular example below

PATRONYMICS etc.

A married couple with children may be addressed as the parents of the first-born male child. Such address implies closeness and respect on the part of the speaker. The parents of Ashraf would be described and addressed as *'aboo 'ashraf* and *'umm 'ashraf*. Couples without children and even unmarried men may be given honorific parenthood titles such as *'aboo Zayd* (hence the widespread use of such terms for describing PLO figures).

Holders of certain names are traditionally called *'aboo* so-and-so. A man called Muhammad may be styled *Abul-Qasim* (recalling the Prophet Muhammad's son who died in infancy). For Christians a slightly bantering example would be that a Maroun would be styled *'aboo-T-Taa'ifa* ('Father of the Sect', i.e. of the Maronites).

LESSON FOURTEEN
■ PROVERBS

Proverbs are used with great effect in Levantine Arabic – as in all Arabic dialects – and are highly prized as the distillation of collective wisdom and experience. A native English speaker would be wary of using English proverbs, fearing to sound quaint or tendentious or both, but Arabic proverbs are used in all contexts.

The student should note carefully how proverbs are used, and with practice should be able to use them appropriately. But be careful! A foreigner using the proverb 'Tie the donkey where its master tells you to' (i.e. 'Follow the boss's instructions!') once caused a major industrial stoppage, since he seemed to be calling an Arab subordinate a donkey!

The following fifty proverbs have been chosen for their popularity. Where necessary explanation is added. Very distinctive attitudes and particular beliefs or superstitions are shown in Nos 10, 14, 20, 22, 23, 24, 25, 26, 29, 30, 31, 32, 35 to 50.

Text	*Translation*
1 'irshak il- 'abyaD liyawmak il-'aswad	Your white penny for your black day (i.e. Save for a rainy day)
2 'ana fee waadee oo 'inta fee waadee	I am in a valley and you are in a valley (i.e. We are at cross-purposes)
3 'il-jaar 'abl id-daar oo ir-rafee' 'abl iT-Taree'	(Choose) the neighbour before the house and the companion before the way (i.e. Plan ahead – but especially in relation to neighbours)
4 man 9aashar al-qawm 'arba9eena yawman Saara min-hum	Who lives with a tribe forty days becomes one of them (i.e. in praise of harmonizing with surroundings)
5 bukra fil-mishmish	Tomorrow in the apricots (when they ripen) (i.e. scepticism about someone's promises)
6 maa ilee wa laa naa'a wa laa jamal fee-ha	I have no she – or he – camel in it (i.e. Nothing to do with me)
7 'urbuT il-Himaar maHall maa bi'ool lak SaaHibo	Tie the donkey in the place where its owner says to (i.e. Follow the boss's instructions)
8 min taHt id-dalaf li-taHt il-mizraab	From under the drip to under the water spout (i.e. From the frying pan into the fire)
9 'imsik il-khashab!	Touch wood!
10 il-manHoos manHoos wa-law 9alla'oo 9alayh faanoos	A chronically unlucky (be-witched) person remains so even if they hang a lamp on him (NB the concept of *naHs* – being bewitched or jinxed – is common in Arabic society)
11 9aash man shaafak	He who sees you lives (very acceptable flattery)

Text	*Translation*
12 khayr ul-birri 9aajiluhu (*classical*)	The best kindness is that done expeditiously
13 'il-maktoob byin'ara min-9unwaano	The letter can be read from its address (i.e. Some things need no explanation)
14 illee byishlaH teeaabo byubrud	He who takes off his clothes gets cold (i.e. Do not cut yourself off from your (family) group)
15 hayk id-dunya!	That's life!
16 Darbat il-mu9allim bi-'alf Darba	The master's touch is worth a thousand by someone else (i.e. an expression of admiration for good work)
17 mush kull-yawn tislam il-jarra	The jar does not remain whole every time (i.e. Be careful)
18 9aSfoor bil-yad wa laa 9ashara bish-shajara	A bird in the hand is better than ten in the tree
19 bya9mal min il- Habba 'ubba	He makes a dome from a grain (i.e. . . . mountains out of molehills)
20 byusru' il-kuHl min il-9ayn	He (would) steal the *Kohl* from the eye (i.e. an incorrigible or skilled thief)
21 farkh il-biTT 9awwaam	The duck's offspring floats (i.e. Like father like son)
22 danab il-kalb byiDall a9waj	The dog's tail remains bent (i.e. Some people are incorrigible, hopeless cases)
23 maa Hada byita9allam 'illa min keeso	No one learns except from his bag/pocket (i.e. Experiences can come dearly)
24 il-9ilm fiS-Sighr mitl in-na'sh fil-Hajr	A thing learned when young is like a thing carved in rock
25 il-9aalam ma9al-waa'if	The world is with the one who is standing (i.e. Might is right)

	Text	*Translation*
26	'illee eedo bil-mayy mush mitl 'illee eedo bin-naar	He whose hand is in the water is not like the one whose hand is in the fire (i.e. It's easy to criticize when you're not facing the tough decisions)
27	'illee faat maat	What has died has passed (i.e. Let bygones be bygones)
28	khaalif tu9raf	Disagree, you become well-known (i.e. disapproval of tendentious individuals)
29	mitl il-Hammaam ma'Too9a mayyaato	Like a bath house whose water has been cut off (i.e. Chaos!)
30	baab in-najjaar makhloo9	The carpenter's door is hanging loose (i.e. 'Physician, heal thyself')
31	byiHkee mitl 'aaDee ma9zool	He talks as much as a dismissed judge
32	mitl il-'aTrash fiz-zaffa	Like a deaf man at a wedding (i.e. doesn't know what's going on)
33	man shabb 9ala shee shaab 9alay(h)	He who grows up with something grows old on it (i.e. Most things can become habitual)
34	9uzr 'a'baH min zanbo	An excuse worse than the offence (e.g. 'Sorry, we didn't come. We forgot')
35	fee kull bayt baaloo9	In every house there is a drain/cesspool (i.e. We all have our faults)
36	ghalTat ish-shaaTir bi-'alf ghalTa	The clever man's mistake is equal to a thousand mistakes (i.e. Gifted people should take special care)
37	Darabnee oo baka, saba'nee oo 'ishtaka	He hit me and wept, got in front of me and complained

Text	*Translation*
	(i.e. Some people have all the cheek!)
38 'akram min Haatim (Tay')	More generous than Haatim (the symbol of Bedouin hospitality)
39 'ana 'ameer oo 'inta 'ameer, oo meen byisoo' il-Hameer	I am a Prince, and so are you. Who, then, will drive the donkeys? (i.e. Someone has to do the dirty work)
40 9indal-buToon Daa9at il-9uqool	When it was time for the bellies (food) the minds went astray
41 baTTeekhtayn bi-eed waa-Hida maa byinHamaloo	Two water melons cannot be carried in one hand (i.e. Match the tools to the job)
42 'ib9ad 9an ish-sharr oo ghannee lo	Keep away from evil and sing to it (cynical advice for keeping in well with people and regimes)
43 ba9eed 9an il-9ayn ba9eed 9an il-'alb	Far from the eye, far from the heart (i.e. Out of sight out of mind)
44 it-tikraar byi9aallim il-Himaar	Repetition will teach even a donkey (beware in using this!)
45 ShaHHaad oo byishaariT	A beggar and (yet) he's haggling (i.e. What impudence!)
46 kull shams il-haa maghrib	Every sun has its setting (i.e. Fame and fortune are fleeting)
47 'iS-Sawm bi-la Salaa mitl ir-raa9ee bi-laa 9aSa	Fast without prayer is like a shepherd with no crook
48 'al qaafila taseer wal-kilaab tanbaH	The caravan proceeds while the dogs bark (i.e. contempt of niggling critics)
49 laa yaDurr as-siHaab nabH il-kilaab	The clouds are not harmed by the barking of the dogs

Text	Translation
And, finally, to sum up on the learning of Arabic:	
50 lisaan jadeed 'insaan jadeed	A new language means a new man

LESSON FIFTEEN
COURTESY EXPRESSIONS FOR VARIOUS OCCASIONS

British English must be unique among developed languages in having no agreed response to the phrase, 'Thank you'. By comparison, Levantine Arabic is rich in polite formulae for every occasion. There is a danger, however, that the foreign student may fear that 'courtesy' Arabic is a cabalistic language which only the initiates may master after undergoing years of travail and nameless rites.

This chapter explains usage appropriate to salutations, congratulations, condolences etc. From the ten sections covered it will be seen that certain phrases are common to many occasions, in particular, invocation to the Deity. The name of *allaah* is used on most occasions and, indeed, 'God bless you' (*allaah yisallimak*) is possibly the most frequently used courtesy formula.

Greetings and welcomes

The Arab gives and expects a warm welcome.

Arabic	Translation	Remarks
1 'ahlan wa sahlan!	Welcome!	A classical phrase: '(You) have come to (your) people and level ground.' Reply: *feek/feeki/feekum*.

Arabic	Translation	Remarks
2 kayf il-Haal? kayf iS-SiHHa?	How are you? How is the health?	Reply: *il-Hamdu lillaah!* ('Praise be to God!') For *kayf* many speakers use *shlawn* (*shlawn SiHHatak?*).
3 marHaba!	Hullo! (a misleading word with complex connotations)	Used by either party in a chance or formal encounter. The root (r–H–b) implies 'Welcome'. Reply: *marHabtayn!* or *maraaHib!*
4 SabaaH il-khayr!	Good morning!	Lit. 'Morning of well-being'. Reply: *SabaaH in-noor* ('Morning of light').
5 masaa il-khayr!	Good evening!	Meaning *and* changes as in 4.
6 nahaarak sa9eed!	May your day be happy!	Used at any time of day. Reply: *nahaarak 'as-9ad* ('. . . happier!')
7 as-salaam 9alaykum!	Peace be upon you!	Used by Muslims. Reply: *wa 9alaykum as-salaam!*

Introductions

1 baHibb 9arrifak 9ala . . .	I'd like to introduce you to . . .	
2 tasharrafna	We are honoured (after being introduced)	NB 'we', not 'I'. Reply: the same or *allaah yizeedak sharaf* ('May God increase your honour').
3 furSa sa9eeda!	A happy occasion!	Reply: *furSa 9aZeema!* ('A great occasion!')

Thanks

1 shukran/ash-kurak/ mutashakkir	Thank you	Reply: *il-9afoo!* ('I beg pardon').

Arabic	*Translation*	*Remarks*
2 mamnoonak	I am obliged to you	Reply: as in 1.
3 'ana 9aajiz 9an ish-shukr	I am quite unable to express my thanks	An acceptable exaggeration. Reply: as above or *laa shukran 9ala waajib* ('No thanks needed for a duty').

Journeys

1 'aymta sharraft?	When did you arrive?	Lit. 'When did you honour us?'
2 'aymta btitsahhil?	When do you leave?	Lit. 'When do you go on a journey which God, we hope, will make easy?'
3 Hamdillaah 9as-salaama	Praise God for your safety	To someone back from a trip. Reply: *allaah yisallimak!*
4 inshallaah tawaffa't bi-hal mishwaar	If God wills you were successful on this trip	Reply: as in 3.
5 inshallaah tarooH oo tirja9 bis-salaama	If God wills you will go and come back in safety	Reply: as in 3.
6 ishta'naalak	We have missed you	To someone returning. Reply: *'iHna bil-'aktar* ('We have missed you more').

Weddings

1 mabrook!	Congratulations!	Lit. 'May you be blessed!' Used to bride and groom, and even parents. Reply: *allaah yisallimak!*
2 inshallaah titahannoo	If God wills you will be made happy	

Funerals

	Arabic	Translation	Remarks
1	allaah yirHamo	May God have mercy on him	
2	il-9awD bi-salaam-tak	The consolation is that you are well	Reply: *allaah yisallimak.*

Departures

1	ma9 is-salaama	(Go) with safety	Reply: *allaah yisallimak.*
2	tuSbaH 9ala khayr	May you arise in the morning in well-being	(Said at night by person leaving.) Reply: *oo 'int min 'ahlo* ('And you are of its family!').

Visit to a sick person

1	salaamtak	(We wish for) your well-being	Reply: *allaah yisallimak. Salaamtak* (with appropriate endearments) would be used on arrival and departure.
2	salaamat-ha	(We wish for) her well-being	Reply: *allaah yisallimak.*

Food and drink etc.

1	bil-'afraaH!	Rejoicing and celebrations!	Used after being entertained. Reply: *allaah yisallimak.*
2	sufra dayima!	May your table last for ever!	Said to a host. Reply: *allaah yideem Hayaatak!* ('May God lengthen your life!')
3	dayima!	Always!	After coffee. Reply: as in 2.
4	na9eeman	May it be pleasant to you	To someone freshly shaved, bathed etc. Reply: *allah yin9am 9alayk!*

Festivals

	Arabic	Translation	Remarks
1	kull 9aam wa 'int bi-khayr	Every year and may you be well	Used for any annual feast, civil or religious, birthdays etc. Reply: *oo 'int bi-khayr.*
2	9eed sa9eed!	A happy feast!	Reply: *allaah yisallimak!*
3	9eed mubaarak!	A blessed feast!	Reply: *allaah yisallimak!*

Conclusion

The above phrases are but a fraction of the possibilities, but will take the student a long way. With increasing familiarity he will pick up variants and additions. It should be noted that, of course, many of the above will need the addition of names or titles or patronymic (see Lesson thirteen on terms of address). Again, much variety is to be expected as between the many communities making up Levant society.

Much more detail on courtesy expressions of the Levant will be found in H. T. Farha's manual (see Bibliography).

The student should be ready to be generous with expressions of courtesy, remembering the common Arabic phrase, 'Anyone who greets you, return his greeting twice over.'

LESSON SIXTEEN
A STORY

'COLLOQUIAL ARABIC'

fee yawm min il-'ayyaam kaan fee ingleezee 'aja lil-bilaad min shaan yata9allam 9arabee. sajjal 'ismo fee madrasat 'il-lughaat fee waSaT 'il-9aaSima oo ballash yudrus il-lugha 'il-9arabiyya il-fuSHa, oo kamaan 'il-9aamiyya. ba9d 'usboo9 shaafoo 'inno mush 9am byita-'addam abadan. maa kaan ya9rif yuktub wa laa yi'raa. oo bin-nisba lil-Hakee ma 'adar yulfuZ Hatta 'absaT il-kalimaat. li has-sabab shaaf mudeer il-madrasa 'inno laazim yighayyir il-barnaamaj shwayy, min shaan yisaa9id ish-shabb il-miskeen. Haraam 'inno yeejee min lundun oo yidfa9 Ha'', tazkirat iT-Tayyaara oo rusoom il-madrasa bil-iDaafa li-takaaleef kull yawm, ya9nee Ha'', il-'akl wash-shurb wan-nawm oo ba9d kull haada maa yita9allam shee! fa, il-mudeer ittafa' ma9 il-'ustaaz taba9o 9ala taghyeer il-barnaamaj 9ala asaas tark il-fuSHa wat-tarkeez 9alal-9aamiyya.

jarraboo il-barnaamaj il-jadeed shahr kaamil, bass . . . bidoon faa'ida. 'ish-shabb maa ta9allam . . . 'ool, maa ta9allam shee, maa 'adir yiHkee 'aktar min kalimatayn, talaata. Ha'ee'a, 9arabee mukassar tamaaman. il-'ustaaz raja9 lil-mudeer oo 'aal lo.

'yaa HaDrat il-mudeer, tismaH lee a'ool lak: hash-shabb il-ingleezee 'illee 9indee biS-Saff maa byiswa bil-marra, 'aHsan yirja9 li-balado. maa feesh faa 'ida, 'abadan. law Dall kamaan 9ishreen sana bil-madrasa mush mumkin yita9allam yiHkee 9arabee! Saddi'nee!'

'Tayyib, ba 'addir maw'ifak, bass shoo na9mal?'

'ana ba'ool lak shoo. 9indee i'tiraaH. inshallaah byi9jabak.'

'tafaDDal! baHibb usaa9ido, miskeen.'

'laysh maa nattafi' ma9 naas, yu'9ud 9ind-hum sitt ush-hur 'aw sana oo maa yiHkee ma9hum illaa 9arabee. hayk laazim yita9allam, ghaSban 9anno!'

'fikra mumtaaza, bass wayn? bta9rif Hada?'

'na9am 9indee 'arayyib saakineen fee shimaal il-bilaad, yimkin 'arba9 meet meel min hawn. jamaa9a kabeera, ikteer Tayyibbeen, oo maa fee wa laa waaHid min-hum bya9rif ingleezee.'

'9aal! mumkin tdabbir Taree'a min shaan yu'9ud 9ind-hum? oo mnidfa9-lum illee laazim . . . oo mnshoof.'

'mnattakil 9alallaah!' oo ba9dayn ittafa'oo ma9 'ahl il 'ustaaz. oo hum ista'baloo ish-shabb fiD-Day9a oo dabbaroo lo ghurfatayn fee bayt 'ibn 9amm il-'ustaaz. haada HaSal fee 'aakhar is-sana oo ba9d sitt 'ush-hur, ya9nee fiS-Sayf, mudeer il-mad-rasa ba9at il-'ustaaz liD-Day9a min shaan yis 'al 9an ish-shabb oo yishoof 'iza biddo shee.

ba9d saa9a biT-Tayyaara oo saa9atayn bil-baaS il-iZgheer illee byimshee 9alal-khaTT bayn iD-Day9a oo markaz il-muHaafaZa il-'ustaaz waSal Haamid shaakir li-'awwal iD-Day9a. lamma nazal min il-baaS shaaf fallaaH 9am byishtaghil Hadd iT-Tareeq. sallam 9alay(h) oo Saar yiHkee ma9o.

'ahlan! ya9Teek il-9aafya!'

'allah yizeedak 9aafya, yaa ustaaz! ahlan wa sahlan! kayf Haal janaabak?'

'allaah yiHfaZak! kayf SiHHatak?'

'nushkur allaah kull saa9a! tfaDDal, ustaaz, 'u9ud shway!'

''afDalt, bass Habbayt 'ukammil iT-Taree liD-Day9a oo ashoof 'ahlee oo Sadee 'ee. yimkin ta9rifo, il-ingleezee 'illee aja la-hawn 'abl sitt 'ush-hur ta'reeban.'

'ma9loom, ba9rifo!'

'wayno halla'?'

'He's just round the corner in the fish-and-chip shop!'

TRANSLATION

Once, there was an Englishman who came to the (this) country to learn Arabic. He registered (his name) at the School of Languages in the centre of the capital and began to study classical Arabic as well as colloquial. A week later they saw that he was not making any progress at all. He could not pronounce even the simplest words. For this reason the director of the school saw that it was necessary to amend the programme (syllabus) a little in order to help the unfortunate young man. (It was) a shame that he should come from London and pay the expense of an air ticket as well as the school fees in addition to daily expenses, that is, the cost of food, drink and accommodation (sleep), and (then) after all this not learn a thing! So the director agreed with his teacher on changing the syllabus, on the basis of abandoning classical (Arabic) and concentrating on colloquial.

They tried the new syllabus for a whole month but with no success (without benefit). The young man learned . . . (well . . . let's) say he learned nothing. He could speak no more than 2 or 3 words. (And) really (it was) completely broken Arabic. The teacher went back to the director and said to him,

'Director, allow me to tell you: this young Englishman who is with me in the class is completely useless. It's better for him to go back to his country. It's (absolutely) no use at all. If he were to stay twenty years more in the school it would be impossible for him to learn to speak Arabic, believe me!'

'Well, I appreciate the position you're in. But what can we do?'

'I'll tell you what. I have a suggestion. I hope it is to your liking.'

'Please go ahead. I want to help him, poor chap.'

'Why don't we make an arrangement with (some) people for him to stay (sit) with them for six months or a year and speak nothing but Arabic with them? In that way (thus) he must learn, in spite of himself!'

'An excellent idea. But where? Do you know anyone?'

'Yes. I have relatives living in the country, maybe 400 miles from here. (They are) a large group, very nice (people), and there's not a single one of them knows English.'

'Wonderful. Can you arrange a way for him to stay with them? We will pay them what is necessary. Then . . . (Well), we'll see.'

'We will rely on God!'

Then they made an agreement with the teacher's family, who received the young man in the village and arranged two rooms for him in the house of the teacher's cousin.

This happened at the end of the year, and six months later, that is, in the summer, the director of the school sent the teacher to the village to enquire about the young man and see if he needed anything.

After an hour in the aircraft and two hours in the small bus which runs between the village and the centre for the province the teacher arrived, praising God and thanking Him, at the beginning of the village.

When he got off the bus he saw a peasant working at the side of the road. He greeted him and began to speak with him.

'Hello! May God give you the fitness!'

'May God increase you in strength sir! Welcome! How are you (Your Honour)?'

'We thank God every hour! Won't you sit down for a while, sir?'

'Thank you but I wanted to finish my journey (complete the way) to the village and see my family and my friend. Maybe you know him, the Englishman who came here about six months ago?'

'Of course I know him!'

'Where is he now?'

'He's just round the corner in the fish-and-chip shop!'

LESSON SEVENTEEN
A MISCELLANY

Of learning languages there is no end. There are always deeper levels to fathom even in one's own language, let alone in a foreign language, to say nothing of a language from a different family, in this case the Semitic family.

The student will always be learning Arabic. There is always more to learn, but this is no cause for despair: the same is true of every language. It is in this sense that all languages are equally difficult. In this chapter fifteen miscellaneous topics are taken which constantly crop up in everyday communication in Arabic, and with which the student should have some familiarity. Some relate to syntax and idiom, others are sociological, anthropological, religious, historical, etymological or morphological.

1 Simple as A, B, C

Arabic uses *abjad, hawaz* etc. for A, B, C. . . . The letters of the alphabet are taken and made into words which sound like genuine Arabic words. These are *abjad, hawaz, HuTTee, kalman, sa9fas, qurshit, thakhadha, DaZagha*.

Furthermore each letter in classical Arabic is assigned numerical value (1–1,000) as follows (*read from right to left*):

أ	ب	ج	د	هـ	و	ز	ح	ط	ي
1	2	3	4	5	6	7	8	9	10

ك	ل	م	ن	س	ع	ف	ص	ق
20	30	40	50	60	70	80	90	100

ر	ش	ت	ث	خ	ذ	ض	ظ	غ
200	300	400	500	600	700	800	900	1,000

'From A to Z' in Arabic is *min al-'alif lil-yaa*.

2 Times of prayer

The Muslim times of prayer are often used as approximate reference points in time. These are: *al fajr*—dawn; *aD-Duhr*—noon; *al-9aSr*—late afternoon; *al-maghreb*—sunset; *al 9isha*—evening prayer.

3 Basic religious terms

Islamic

(a) The Five Pillars of Islam

    (i) *shahaada*: to testify that 'There is no God but God and Muhammad is the Prophet of God' (*laa 'illaaha 'illallaahu wa muHammad rasoolu-llaah*).

    (ii) *Salaat*: prayer, five times daily as in 2 above.

    (iii) *zakaat*: alms-giving.

    (iv) *Hajj*: pilgrimage to Mecca in the pilgrimage month.

    (v) *Sawm*: fast of the month of Ramadan.

(b) Names for the Koran (a small selection)

    (i) *'al-muSHaf* (the Book).

    (ii) *'al-qur'aan al-kareem* (the noble Koran).

    (iii) *aS-SiraaT al-mustaqeem* (the straight path).

    (iv) *adh-dhikru-l-Hakeem* (the wise mention of God).

(c) Four law-codes in Sunni Islam

    (i) Hanafi.

    (ii) Hanbali.

    (iii) Shafa'i.

    (iv) Maliki.

(d) Phrases used following the names of celebrated figures in Islam.

    (i) Muhammad: *9alay(h) aS-Salaat was-salaam* ('May prayers and peace be upon him').

    (ii) Each of the first four Caliphs: *raDee allaah 9anhu* ('May God be pleased with him').

    (iii) Many other heroic and/or holy figures: *karram allaah wajhahu* ('May God honour his face').

Christian

(a) Church—*kaneesa*; priest—*khooree*; mass—*'uddaas*; bishop—*'us'uf* or *muTraan*; baptism ceremony—*9imaada*; sect—*Taa'ifa*.

(b) *Sects*. Roman Catholic—*laateen*; Greek Orthodox—*room*; Greek Catholic—*room kaatooleek*; Protestant—*brootestant*. And many others.

4 Calendar months

AD *(Christian)* (Jan., Feb. etc.)	AH *(Muslim)*
1 kaanoon taanee	muHarram
2 shbaaT	Safar
3 'aadaar	rabee9 il-awwal
4 neesaan	rabee9 it-taanee
5 'ayyaar	jumaada il-oola
6 Huzayraan	jumaada il-'aakhira
7 tammooz	rajab
8 'aab	shawwaal
9 'aylool	ramaDaan
10 tishreen 'awwal	sha9baan
11 tishreen taanee	dhool-qa9da
12 kaanoon 'awwal	dhool-Hijja

The two calendars do not coincide, of course: the Islamic calendar is lunar and is of 354 days, the months having twenty-nine or thirty days, alternately. The Christian calendar corresponds to the Gregorian calendar.

5 Trades and professions

The pattern –*a*– (doubled) *aa*– indicates 'one professionally engaged on some activity'.
Hence:

baker—khabbaaz	mason—Hajjaar
butcher—laHHaam	tentmaker—khayyaam
carpenter—najjaar	blacksmith—Haddaad
money changer—Sarraaf	coppersmith—naHHaas

6 Colours

The principal colours are all of the pattern *'a--a-* (f. *-a--aa*).

red—'aHmar (*pl.* Humr)   black—'aswad (*pl.* sood)
white—'abyaD (*pl.* beeD)   green—'akhDar (*pl.* khuDr)
blue—'azra' (*pl.* zur')   yellow—'aSfar (*pl.* Sufr)
brown—'asmar (*pl.* sumr)

Feminines are of the pattern *'aHmar/Hamraa* (hence the Alhambra in Spain).

Other colours

brown—bunnee (*coffee-coloured*)   pink—wardee (*rose-coloured*)

7 Shapes, areas etc.

Triangle—muthallath   circle—daa'ira
square—murabba9   cube—muka99ab

8 Numbers, powers etc.

odd number—9adad fardee
even number—9adad zawjee
a pair of shoes—zawj (jawz) kundara
a dozen—darzen
bilateral—thunaa'ee
trilateral—thulaathee
quadrilateral (quartet, quatrain)—rubaa9ee (e.g. *of Omar Khayyam*)
five-fold (quintet)—khumaasee
six-fold (sextet)—sudaasee
seven-fold (septet)—subaa9ee
eight-fold (octet)—thumaanee
nine-fold (nonet)—tusaa9ee
ten-fold—'9ushaaree

Notice another pattern giving useful numerical ideas. From *thalaatha* comes *muthallath* (triangle). Hence:

muthanna—dual (grammar)
muthallath—triangle
murabba9—square
mukhammas—pentagon
musaddas—hexagon (but also 'revolver' i.e. 'six-shooter'!)

9 What's in a name?

Whereas English does not now use names such as Praise-the-Lord Barebones, Arabic names always tell a story.

(a) Origins

Many family names are based on the place of origin: hence Hourani, Shami, Trabulsi, Halabi, Nabulsi (to use American names of Levantine origin).

(b) Qualities

Many personal names describe virtues.

kareem—generous   SaaliH—upright
saleem—sound   najeeb—of good stock
fareed—unique   naseeb—of noble descent

(There are many proverbs and stories illustrating discrepancy between a name and its owner's qualities!)

(c) Qualities to be avoided!

Names expressing defects may relate to the condition of an eponymous ancestor, or may be given to ward off the affliction referred to.

'aTrash—deaf   'a9war—one-eyed

(d) Trades and professions

(See section 5 above.)

Haddaad—blacksmith   najjaar—carpenter

(e) Religious names

(i) The largest category of names is that beginning with Abdul (*9abdul-*). This means 'the slave of . . .', but the name is incomplete without the addition of one of the ninety-nine *Most Beautiful Names* of God. Hence:

9abdul-9azeez, 9abdul-kareem, 9abdul-majeed, 9abdul-waaHid

Although this group of names is usually given to Muslim males, some Christians have names of this kind, either as personal or family names. Abdullah (*9abdullaahi*) is used by both Christians and Muslims.

(ii) Some names are clearly always Muslim: Muhammad, Ali, Hussayn etc.

(iii) The Shia tend to prefer certain names over others: Ali, Hassan, Hussayn.

10   Religious festivals (selected)

Christian	*Muslim*
Christmas—9eed il-meelaad	Prophet's Birthday—mawlid in-nabee
Good Friday—al-jum9a al-Hazeena	Muhammad's miraculous journey—il-mi9raaj
Easter—9eed il-fiSH	Hijra New Year—'awwal muHarram
Whit Sunday—9eed il-9anSara	End of Ramadan—9eed il-fiTr
Ascension—9eed iS-Su9ood	Hajj Feast—9eed il-'aDHa

11   The feminine 'it'

As in many other languages a vaguely defined 'it' is rendered in the feminine (cf. English, 'You've had it!', 'It's a mess!'). Below are examples in Levantine colloquial.

   (i)   bifrij-haa 'allaah!—God will sort it out!
   (ii) Tuli9at 'inno . . .—It turned out that . . .
  (iii) mndabbir-haa—We'll fix things.
  (iv) maa Tuli9at bi-eedo—He failed (lit. 'It did not come up into his hand')

(v)   saa'abat inno . . .—It just happened that . . .
(vi) khallee-haa 9alaynaa—This one's on me (e.g. restaurant
        bill)
(vii) maa btifri' ma9ee—It makes no difference to me
(viii) takhkhanoo-haa—They overdid it/went too far
(ix) halla' ZabaTat—*Now* it's turned out OK
(x)   maa misheet—Things did not go well (lit. 'It did not
        walk')
(xi) 'akaloo-haa—They had a terrible time (lit. 'They ate it')
(xii) wa't-haa, saa9at-haa, yawmit-haa—at that time, then
(xiii) mleeH innha maa kaanat 'a9Zam—A good thing things
        were no worse
(xiv) bi-laa-haa—Never mind, forget it!
(xv) 9am bitshattee—It's raining

12   The future negative

A common pattern is:

We shall not see him—mush Haa-nshoofo
Won't you be coming?—mush Haa-teejee?

Haa is a truncated form of the colloquial future particle *raaH*.

13   Present tense negative

'He is not . . .' is frequently rendered in the Levant (especially
Lebanon) by *maano(h)sh*. This is (a) the negative *maa*, plus (b) the
particle *inn*, plus (c) the pronoun, plus (d) the negative suffix */sh/*.
Hence:

He is not here—maano(h)sh mawjood

The other pronouns may be substituted.

14   The double-possessive/object pronoun

A very common Lebanese formula is as follows:

Karim's book—kitaabo la-kareem
Samira's husband—jawz-haa la-sameera
He hit Samir—Darabo la-sameer

15 **'Arabic has no word for "interesting"'**[*]

To round off this miscellany, the above myth should be finally laid to rest.

What is true is that the English word 'interesting' does duty for many words, even 'boring' (e.g. 'How interesting!'). 'An interesting condition/person/book/evening/idea' can all be rendered perfectly adequately in Arabic, but no one word covers all the above cases. Among translations for 'interesting' are *mufeed*, *muhimm*, *lazeez*, *shayyi'*, *mushawwi'* and *mutheer lil-ihtimaam*.

The student can judge the quality of English–Arabic dictionaries by the number of Arabic words given for 'interesting'.

LESSON EIGHTEEN
CONCEPTS IN SOCIETY

'Let us pause to consider the . . . Levantines' – as Ogden Nash might have said.

The Levant Arabic-speaking population includes a wide variety of Christian sects (Uniate and Orthodox divisions of all the principal Eastern communities, together with Roman Catholics and Protestants of many persuasions) in addition to the predominantly Sunni Muslim population. Of other Muslim communities there are many varieties: Shia ('Seveners' and 'Twelvers'), Druze, Nusairis (Alawites) etc. Then there are small communities of Arabic-speaking Jews, not to mention members of the Bahai and other communities.

Since adherence to religious community is of fundamental importance in the Levant (e.g. conflicts in 1979 in Syria between Sunni and Alawite; the constitution of the Lebanese parliament, Christian and Muslim in the ratio of 6 to 5; the name of the kingdom of Jordan, 'Hashemite'), it is not surprising that evidence of adherence to community is found in speech. Indeed it is this area

---

[*]'cannot be adequately expressed in Arabic': J. van Ess, *The Spoken Arabic of Iraq*, 2nd edn, Oxford, 1938, p. 162.

which gave the word *shibboleth* to the English language: possibly the most famous example in world history of betrayal of community origins and belief by a single word (see the Introduction).

The student should realize that knowledge of Arabic implies not only knowledge of syntax and pronunciation but an awareness of the dimension of *concepts*, i.e. the basic assumptions about society which underlie the native speaker's use of his language. Religion is only one element, though a very obvious one: a Muslim may, in an everyday 'oath', invoke the Prophet Muhammad, while a Christian may invoke the Cross. The student will also come across ideas more or less unfamiliar to him (depending on his own origins) relating to family relationships, the constituent elements of society, neighbours, what makes life worth living, the hereafter, sex, time, the position of women, marriage, race, superstition, honour, politics, fate, birth, life and death.

This lesson explains some of the language used in relation to some of these concepts. A beginning may be made as follows.

Oaths

By comparison with British English, Levantine Arabic is extremely rich in oaths. Whereas in the author's lifetime 'By God!' and 'By Jove!' have declined in British use, Levantine speech has maintained its traditional everyday oaths. A man may give extra emphasis to a statement by saying:

1 wallaahee (il-9aZeem)!—By Almighty God! (Largely Muslim)
2 wa-Hyaat 'oolaadee!—By the life of my children!
3 wa-Hyaat in-nabee!—By the life of the Prophet! (Muslim)
4 wa-Hyaat il-maseeH!—By the life of Jesus the Messiah! (Christian)
5 wa-Hyaat 9uyoonee!—By the life of my eyes!
6 bi-sharafee!—By my honour!
7 wa-Hyaat il-'imaam 9alee—By the life of the Imam Ali! (Shia)
8 wa-Hyaat haadol . . . (ish-shawaarib/il-9uyoon)!—By the life of these . . . moustaches/eyes!
9 wa-Hyaat il-9adraa!—By the life of the Virgin! (Christian)
10 wa-Hyaat 9arDee!—By the life of my honour!

Honour

sharaf and *9arD* are used. The first tends to refer to generalized personal or family standing, while the second has complex implications, frequently to do with the honour of a family group *as represented by its women-folk* (cf. T. Y. Awwad's novel *Death in Beirut*, Heinemann Educational Books, London, 1976, translated by the present writer). In a famous incident, however, a Lebanese community leader was in modern times presented at his front door with the head of a follower's sister with the words: *ghasalna ish-sharaf* ('We have washed clean the (family) honour').

Fate

It was written—maktoob!
It was a judgment of God and fate—qaDaa oo qadar!

Groups in society

Muslims (usage by non-Muslims)—il-'islaam
my ancestors (grandfathers)—'ujdoodee
my uncles (paternal)—9umoomtee
    (maternal)—'akhwaalee
our group (can mean family or even religious community)—
  jamaa9atnaa

What makes life worth living

Clearly an enormously broad field but any foreigner must be familiar with a key phrase: *keef oo basaT*, approximately 'good spirits and cheer'.

Time

As is well known by rumour, the Arab's approach to time is, at least, more flexible than that of non-Arabs. Two phrases may be examined to illustrate possible misunderstandings.

bukra is frequently taken by foreigners to mean 'tomorrow'. To a Levantine it may, quite sincerely, mean only 'at some time in the future'. Indeed in Lebanon they say *bukra 9aa-bukra* for 'to-morrow'.

fee hal-yawmayn – lit. 'in these (next) two days'. Frequently the Levantine means by this (apparently exact) phrase only 'quite soon'.

Women

Care must be taken to use the right term of reference or address. Among phrases to be heard are:

is-sitt—the lady (i.e. your wife)
sitt-haanum—madame (with a Turkish honorific)
madaamtak—your wife (Lebanese, indeed Beiruti!)
martee—my wife (some groups would deplore this usage)
il-Hurma—my wife (used in very conservative circles, e.g. among Bedu)
il-maHroosa—your daughter (lit. 'the guarded one')
mart-9ammee—my mother-in-law (lit. 'the wife of my uncle'). NB A euphemism is felt to be needed!

Marriage and divorce

The subject is so fundamental and attitudes are so varied that refuge will be sought in brevity!

1 'Divorce' is *Talaa'*. A Muslim divorce ('I divorce thee' said three times) is *'iT-Talaa' bit-talaata*. A bantering oath used to persuade someone to do something is: 'I will divorce my wife!' *baTalli' martee*.

But note that *Talla't-haa* can mean not only 'I divorced her' but 'we parted company', e.g. two unmarried people. (The root T–1–' means 'be free'.)

2 NB a very revealing word:

He married X's daughter—*'akhad bint fulaan* (*lit. 'He took X's daughter'*)

3 *Honeymoon*. The phrase is an exact rendering of *lune de miel* or 'honeymoon': *shahr il-9asl* ('month of honey'). The phrase used for the wedding night is less ambiguous: *laylat id-dakhla*, lit. 'the night of the entering'.

Race/community

Every community throughout the world likes to distinguish itself from others by developing its own terms for referring to others: hence 'ethnic' jokes and terms such as 'paddies', 'jocks', 'limeys' etc. Levant society has its 'ethnic' jokes, though they tend to be directed against the next village rather than against other countries. A certain village in Lebanon refers to the next two villages in rhyming prose as follows: 'If it weren't for—and—the world would be empty of morons'. Two phrases which should be cleared up are:

1   il-9arab—lit. 'the Arabs'
Depending on who says it, this may mean 'non-Lebanese', 'the Bedu' or 'member states of the Arab League'.

2   il-9abeed—lit. 'the slaves'
This apparently offensive phrase is commonly used of blacks, even of US citizens. It is best regarded as being like English titles such as Tory, which were originally terms of abuse but have now more or less lost their pejorative connotations.

Superstition

Levantine society has inherited a wealth of ideas which seem to be irreconcilable with the degree of scientific education attained by their adherents. Belief in 'the evil eye' is very widespread, and the consultation of fortune tellers was attributed to 80 per cent of the population of Lebanon in a survey in the late 1960s. Two common phrases may illustrate this.

1   ba9eed 9annak—far from you
This is used to wish that the interlocutor may not be affected by the unpleasant thing just mentioned: death, disease etc.

2   yikhza-l-9ayn—'may He disgrace the (evil) eye'
This phrase may be used to express admiration for a handsome child. NB In most Levantine societies it is not usual or welcome for such admiration to be explicitly formulated, so as not to attract the evil eye.

Family reputation

It is difficult to exaggerate the importance of a family's reputation. A term of admiration is *ibn-naas*: 'a son of people', i.e. of people of standing. To preserve a family's standing periodic clan-gatherings are common: a well-known *Baalbek* (Lebanon) extended family claims 22,000 members.

Revenge

Not only the Bedu insist on revenge; vendettas are endemic throughout the Levant.

To take revenge — il-'akhd bit-taar (*CA* tha'r)

Influence

To end on a lighter note, all should be aware of the need for *waaSTa*, lit. 'mediation'.

In a society accustomed to leader–client relationships, modern impersonal bureaucracy is intrusive. Dealings with government are regarded as so fraught with perils that reliance can be placed only on those known to the petitioner/citizen to have influence. Hence the frequency of appeals for intervention made to 'Godfather' figures for assistance in getting passports, telephones and permits of all kinds.

LESSON NINETEEN
ABUSE

A delicate subject!
1 It is inviting trouble to attempt to instruct a foreigner on how to be abusive.
2 Below are examples of expressions which may be heard. These are given for purposes of *comprehension* only. There is no

recommendation to use any of these phrases, still less to reply to them!

3   The town of Zahle in the Lebanon is famous for the richness and inventiveness of the terms of abuse used by its inhabitants.

4   Care should be taken in attempting to be equally innovative.

Term	Meaning	Remarks
1 Hayawaan!	Animal!	Often heard between cab-drivers.
2 'ibn kalb!	Son of a dog!	Lack of remarks in this column should be interpreted as a silently eloquent injunction to *be careful!*
3 Himaar!	Donkey!	Often rounded out with *'ibn-Himaar!*
4 yil9an deenak!	May your religion be cursed!	His/your/their, etc.
5 yil9an 'abook!	May your father be cursed!	Extreme caution!
6 yil9an deen 'aboo(h)!	May his father's religion be cursed!	
7 yukhrab baytak!	May your house be destroyed!	yukhrab bayto! shoo Tayyib!('. . . What a good man!') is a common paradox, used amicably.
8 ibn-sharmooTa!	Son of a whore!	Other kinship terms possible!
9 yu'Suf 9umro!	May his life be blasted!	See 7 above for use as a term of praise.
10 yiHri' deeno!	May his religion be burned!	See 7 above for use as a term of praise.
11 9akroot!	Pimp!	
12 9ars!	Pimp!	
13 ibn wuskha!	Son of an unclean woman!	See 8 above.

Term		*Meaning*
14	ghabee!	Idiot!
15	baheem!	Bovine creature!
16	bighl!	Mule!
17	tees!	Moron!
18	fallaaH!	Peasant!
19	ibn Haraam!	Bastard!
20	yaa 'aleel il-'adab	Uncivilized

The above twenty expressions are, it is repeated, given for reference and comprehension purposes only. The student will find more detail in H. T. Farha (see Bibliography).

PART TWO
APPENDICES

KEY TO EXERCISES

LESSON ONE

1 The boy is English
2 The girl is French
3 The book is an Arabic book
4 The girl's book is here
5 The teacher's daughter is here
6 mu9allim il-walad 'ajnabee
7 abnaa il-'ajnabee hawn
8 'il-walad il-amreekaanee 'ibn il-mu9allim
9 'iHna abnaa il-mu9allim il-'ingleezee
10 'il-bint is-sooriyya bint is-safeer

LESSON TWO

1 He is in the teacher's room
2 The two girls are with my teacher
3 The big man is from Amman
4 I have two girls and a boy
5 She has her new book
6 9indo sayyaara jadeeda (or 'ijdeeda)
7 hiya ma9o fil-ghurfa il-kabeera (or il-ikbeera)
8 hum kull-hum ma9na hawn
9 kull-na ingleez
10 kull-hum 'ajaanib

Appendix

1 How many weeks are there in a year?
2 There are 120 minutes in two hours
3 How old is he? He is six months
4 The boy is ten
5 fish-shahr il-hijree fee tis9a oo 9ishreen aw talaateen yawm
6 He has twenty books
7 They have four cars
8 I have thirty Syrian lira
9 She has forty-five Jordanian dinars
10 The year 1914
11 9indee talaat sayyaaraat ijdeeda
12 ma9haa talaata oo khamseen leera lubnaanee
13 ma9ak talaata oo talaateen deenaar urdunee?
14 (tilifoon) 'arba9miyya oo tis9a oo khamseen; tis9amiyya oo
    sab9a oo talaateen
15 Sanat 'alf oo tis9amiyya oo tis9a oo talaateen

LESSON THREE

1 They took with them 130 newspapers
2 Who opened this door?
3 When did you (f. sing.) get to know this book?
4 The schoolboys used maps
5 The foreigners went down from Amman to Jericho
6 haadi khaarTat ish-shaam (dimashq)
7 'akhad-hum kull-hum ma9o 'ila bayroot
8 rajja9oona kull-na min ish-shaam 'ila 9ammaan
9 'akhadoo il-karaasee min madrasatna
10 kaatabto sanat alf oo tis9a miyya oo tamaanya oo khamseen

LESSON FOUR

1 We returned the books before they arrived
2 Open the school gate!
3 Write a letter to the teacher!
4 He introduced us to the ambassador's son
5 This book is better than that, isn't it?
6 laazim yi9arrifoonee 9ala-l-awlaad is-saa9a 'arba9a oo nuSS

7   maa tuktuboo 'aktar min arba9a makaateeb!
8   katab makaateebo ba9d maa waSalnaa
9   bidd-hum yuktuboo makaateeb 'ila 'awlaad-hum
10 raaH tishrabee mayy ma9 'aklik

LESSON FIVE

1   You are living in the other street, aren't you?
2   Prepare the food, please!
3   He is studying the chart of the new offices
4   Come in and shut the door!
5   Why are the children wearing Arab dress?
6   khud hal-makaateeb 'ila madkhal il-maktab is-saa9a 'itnayn oo
      nuSS
7   sami9hum 'abl maa dakhaloo
8   had-dakaakeen faatiHa (maftooHa) is-saa9a sab9a oo nuSS?
9   laazim nishrab shee baarid
10 yimkin yaakuloo shee 'abl is-saa9a khamsa illa rub9

LESSON SIX

1   (Just) between ourselves, don't say a thing tonight!
2   Can you speak colloquial Arabic?
3   No, but I can write Arabic
4   Go and get on with your work! (Lit. '. . . see your work!')
5   Please take away the knife, the forks and the spoons
6   laazim yijeeb kull kutubo ma9o il-yawm
7   biddik titakallamee il-lugha il-9arabiyya il-fuSHa?
8   maa ni'dir narooH ma9kum min 9ammaan 'ila bayroot
9   jeeboo kull shee ma9kum min il-bayt il-taanee!
10 taSawwar! biddo yisheel kull hal kutub!

LESSON SEVEN

1   What did you say to him? I didn't say a thing to him!
2   Where are you going? I'm not going anywhere!
3   That's life! One day for you, another day against you!
4   I want to put these books in the same place
5   No, put them here, with me, please!

6   khalleena nalta'ee bukra 'is-saa9a sab9a illa rub9 masaa'an
7   mush Darooree tarooH 'abl maa tishoofo
8   lamma tiTla9 la-barra tiHmarr!
9   ba9d maa tishoofee-haa rooHee 'ila bayt-ha
10   kull waaHid laazim yihtamm fee shughlo

LESSON EIGHT

1   What's wrong? (lit. 'What is there?') My hand is hurting me
2   He offered to clean the car for me
3   All my friends opposed me when I suggested this idea to them
4   I came to the school because they brought your friends with
        them
5   The car came to a stop in the middle of the city
6   biddak tishoof sayyaarto il-'ijdeeda?
7   maa byinwajad shee mitlo fil-madeena kull-haa
8   Tab9an mush kull 'aSHaabna raaH yooSaloo fee nafs is-saa9a
9   btismaH lee 'uwa ''if is-sayyaara?
10   'iD DaabiT 'a9Taanee hal-kitaab

LESSON NINE

1   Whose is this car?
2   The letter which I put on the table is not here now
3   The girl to whom we were introduced is ten years old
4   They all came into the room where we were meeting ('. . . in
        which . . .')
5   We heard that he is going to Amman in the car which he
        bought in Beirut
6   bta9rif meen ir-rajul 'illee kaanoo yiDHakoo 9alay(h)?
7   la-meen (or taba9 meen) il-kutub 'illee jibt-haa ma9ak?
8   'abl maa tighassil eedayk khallee kutubak hawn
9   maa tiDHak 9alayh, 9am byijarrib
10   meen is-sitt 'illee shuftak ma9haa?

LESSON TEN

1   The life of the peasants is very difficult in winter
2   Where do you spend the summer, in Damascus or in Amman?

3 I (would) prefer that you come any time you are free
4 Foreigners like to come to the country in winter because their
       country is cold ('. . . in it is cold . . .')
5 I saw him coming but I did not have time to stop the car
6 kaanat 9am bitshattee (id-dinya) wa't maa jeet min il-balad
7 fee lubnaan, bitshattee (id-dunya) ikteer fir-rabee9?
8 min faDlak, 'a9Teenee il-ustaaz 'aHmad! ghalaT! (. . . Habee-
       bee!)
9 baajee 'ilal-maktab Haalmaa 'ashoofo
10 btreed teejee fis-sayyaara 'il-ijdeeda 'illee 'ishtaraynaa-haa,
       'ana oo 'aSHaabee?

LESSON ELEVEN

1 Believe me, this is the best book in English on Arabic poetry.
2 Tell me, what time do you finish (your) work?
3 If you go to Amman you (will) find many new hotels
4 If we had been here two years ago we would not have seen a
       single school. Not one (lit. 'at all/ever')
5 If you find a good book in Arabic on French poetry bring it to
       me
6 huwa jaaee min ish-shaam min shaan yudrus iS-SaHaafa fil-
       jaami9a
7 9arift (or btaarif) 'inno SaaHibee mutakhaSSiS fil-baraamij it-
       tarbawiyya?
8 btreed shee ghayro?
9 iza biddak tata9arraf 9alar-rajul 'illee shufto ta9aal 'ila baytee
       bukra is-saa9a tis9a S-Subh
10 Law (kunt) ishtaghalt ma9o (kunt) Sirt milyoonayr

GRAMMAR, INDEXED
BY LESSON

VOCABULARY

A

about (e.g. a subject)—9an

above—faw'

acclimatized: become acclimatized—ta'a'lam (II)

addition: in addition to—bil-'iDaafa 'ila

address (n.)—9unwaan (*pl.* 9anaaween)

administer—'adaar (IV)

aeroplane—Taa'ira (*pl.* -aat), Tayyaara (*pl.* -aat)

afraid: be afraid—khaaf, byikhaaf, khawf

after (conj.)—ba9dmaa

after (prep.)—ba9d

afternoon—ba9d aD-Duhr

age—9umr (*pl.* 'a9maar)

ago (e.g. a year ago)—'abl sana

agree with—'ittafa' ma9

airport—maTaar (*pl.* -aat)

all—kull

allow, permit (to)—samaH, byismaH, samaaH (la)

almsgiving—zakaa(t)

aloud—bi-Sawt 9aalee

already (*see Lesson ten*)

also—kamaan

ambassador—safeer (*pl.* sufaraa')

amend, adjust, alter—ghayyar (II)

American—'amreekaanee (*pl.* 'amreekaan)

among—bayn

ancestors—'ujdood

and—oo, wa

animal—Hayawaan (*pl.* -aat)

ape (e.g.) foreigners—tafarnaj (II)

appreciate—'addar (II)

approach—'arrab (II)

approximately—ta'reeban

apricots—mishmish

Arab, Arabic—9arabee (*pl.* 9arab)

arrange, fix—dabbar (II)

arrive—waSal, byooSal, wuSool

as: as much as you like—'add maa biddak/btreed

Ascension (feast)—9eed aS-Su9ood

ask—sa'al, byis'al, su'aal

assemble (intransitive)—'ijtama9 (VIII)

assist—saa9ad (III)

assistant—musaa9id (*pl.* -een)

author—kaatib (*pl.* kuttaab)

autumn—khareef

available: be available—
tayassar (V)

B

back to front—bil-ma'loob, bil-
'ilb

bag, sack—kees (*pl.* 'akyaas)

baker—khabbaaz (*pl.* -een)

baptism—9imaada

bark (vb)—nabaH, byinbaH,
nab(a)H

bastard (abuse)—9akroot (*pl.*
9akaareet)

bath, 'loo', bath-house—
Hammaam (*pl.* -aat)

bear: I can't bear him—
taHammal (V)

because—li-'ann (*see Lesson
eight*)

become—Saar, byiSeer,
maSeer

beer—beera

before (prep.)—'abl

before (conjunction)—
'ablmaa

beggar—shaHHaad (*pl.* -een)

begin—Saar, byiSeer; ballash
(II); bada', byibda', bidaaya

believe—Sadda' (II)

below—taHt

bent, crooked—'a9waj

best—'aHsan, khayr

better—'aHsan

between, among—bayn

big, large—kabeer (*pl.* kibaar)

bilateral—thunaa'ee

bird—Tayr (*pl.* Tuyoor)

bird (small)—9uSfoor (*pl.*
9aSaafeer)

birthday—9eed meelaad

birthday of the Prophet
Muhammad—mawlid
an-nabee

bishop—'us'uf (*pl.* 'asaa'ifa)

black—'aswad

blacksmith—Haddaad (*pl.*
-een)

blast (vb)—'aSaf, byu'Suf,'aSf

book—kitaab (*pl.* kutub)

boy, son—walad (*pl.* 'awlaad)

bride—9aroos (*pl.* 9urus)

bridegroom—9arees

bring—jaab, byijeeb

bring! (imperative)—haat!

broken—mukassar

broken down, worn out, out of
order—kharbaan

bureau—maktab (*pl.* makaatib)

burn (vb)—Hara', byiHri', Har'

but—walaakin, bass

butcher—laHHaam (*pl.* -een)

buy—'ishtara (VIII)

C

call (out to)—naada (III)

camel—jamal (*pl.* jimaal)

camel (female)—naa'a (*pl.* -aat)

can, be able—'adar, byi'dar,
'udra (*and followed by the
imperative vb; see also Lesson
four*)

car—sayyaara (*pl.* -aat)

caravan—'aafila (*pl.* 'awaafil)

carpenter—najjaar (*pl.* -een)

carve—na'ash, byun'ush, na'sh
cattle—baheem
centre—markaz (*pl.* maraakiz, waSat)
certainly, of course—ma9loom, Tab9an
chair—kursee (*pl.* karaasee)
changed (his mind)—ghayyar (II) (fikro)
cheap—rakheeS
Cheers! (A toast)—SaHHtayn! (*Reply*: 9ala 'albak!)
chick, offspring—farkh (*pl.* firaakh)
Christ—(as-sayyid) al-maseeH
Christian—maseeHee (*pl.* -een)
Christmas—yawm 9eed il-meelaad
church—kaneesa (*pl.* kanaayis)
circle, vicious circle—daa'ira (*pl.* dawaa'ir), Hal'a faarigha
city—madeena (*pl.* mudun)
classical (Arabic)—(al-lugha al-9arabiyya) al-fuSHa
classroom—Saff (*pl.* Sufoof)
clean (adj.)—naZeef (pl. niZaaf)
clean (vb)—naDDaf (II)
clerk—kaatib (*pl.* kataba)
clever—shaaTir
clock—saa9a (*pl.* -aat)
close (vb)—sakkar (II)
clothes—malaabis
clouds—suHub, siHaab
cold—baarid
cold (of persons)—bardaan
colloquial—daarij, 9aammiyya
colour—lawn (*pl.* 'alwaan)
come—'aja byeejee

come back—raja9, byirja9, rujoo9
come near, move—'arrab (II)
community (religious)—Taa'ifa (*pl.* Tawaa'if)
companion—rafee'
complain—'ishtaka (VIII)
concentrate on—rakkaz (II) 9ala
Congratulations!—mabrook!
consult (a book)—raaja9 (III)
correspond with (write to)—kaatab (III)
correspondent—mukaatib (*pl.* -een)
count (vb)—9add, byi9idd, 9add
country—bilaad (*pl.* buldaan)
cousin—ibn 9amm/khaal (*etc.*)
cube—muka99ab
curse (vb)—la9an, byil9an, la9n
cut, cut off—'aTa9, byi'Ta9, 'aT9

D

dark: It became dark—9atamat id-dunya
dawn—fajr
day—yawm (*pl.* 'ayyaam)
deaf—'aTrash
dear (expensive)—ghaalee
dear (endearment)—9azeez
desk—maktab (*pl.* makaatib)
despair (vb)—ya'as, byay'as, ya's
destroy—kharrab (II)

devil; Poor devil!—shayTaan
(*pl.* shayaaTeen); miskeen
(*pl.* masaakeen)

difference: It makes no
difference to me—maa btifri'
ma9ee

different (various)—mukhtalif

difficult—Sa9b

dine—ta9ashsha (V)

director—mudeer (*pl.*
mudaraa)

dirty—wusikh (*pl.* -een)

dismiss, 'fire'—9azal, byi9zal,
9azl

divorce—Talla' (II)

do, make—9 amil, bya9mal,
9aml

dog—kalb (*pl.* kilaab)

dome—'ubba (*pl.* 'ubab)

done: be done—'in9amal

donkey—Himar (*pl.* Hameer)

door, gate—baab (*pl.* 'abwaab)

doubt (vb)—shakk, byishukk,
shakk

doubtless—bi-laa shakk,
bidoon shakk

dozen—darzen

drain, cesspool—baaloo9

drink (n.)—mashroob (*pl.* -aat)

drink (vb)—sharib, byishrab,
shurb

dual (grammar)—muthanna

duck—biTT

during—'asnaa

dwell, live—sakan, byuskun,
sakan

dwelling—maskan (*pl.*
masaakin)

E

each one—kull waaHid

each other; on top of each
other—al-ba9D; faw'
ba9D

early—bakkeer

east—shar'

Easter—9eed al-fiSH

eat—'akal, byaakul, 'akl

education—tarbeea

Egypt—miSr

either . . . or—yaa . . . yaa

employ, use—ista9mal (X)

employee—muwaZZaf

empty—faarigh

end—nihaaya

end of year—'aakhar is-sana

English—'ingleezee (*pl.*
'ingleez)

enter—dakhal, byudkhul,
dukhool

entrance—madkhal (*pl.*
madaakhil)

equals—byisaawee

even (e.g. 'even you')—Hatta

even if—Hatta wa law

evening—masaa

everyone—kull waaHid

evil (n.)—sharr

except (conjunction)—'illaa

excuse (n.)—9udhr (*pl.*
'a9dhaar)

exit—makhraj (*pl.* makhaarij)

expel—'akhraj (IV)

expenses—takaaleef,
maSaareef

express (adj.)—musta9jil

express (vb)—9abbar (II) 9an

extend, stretch—madd,
byimidd, madd

eye—9ayn (*pl.* 9uyoon)

F

face; lose face—wajh (*pl.*
wujooh); fa'ad mayy wajho

fall—wa'a9, byoo'a9, wu'oo9

fall in love with—wa'a9 fee
Hubb (fulaan)

fall out with, quarrel with—
takhaana' (VI) ma9

far, distant—ba9eed (*pl.*
bi9aad)

far from—ba9eed 9an

fast (adj.)—saree9

fast (n.)—Sawm

fast (vb)—Saam, byiSoom,
Siyaam

fate; 'That is fate'—qadr;
qaDaa' wa qadr

father—'ab (*pl.* 'aabaa)

favour: do me a favour—
ma9roof

fcar (n.)—khawf

fear (vb)—khaaf, byikhaaf,
khawf

fed up—zah'aan

feel—sha9ar, byush9ur,
shu9oor; Hass, byiHiss, Hiss

feelings; Are you feeling all
right?—mashaa9ir; Haasis bi-
shee?

fees—rusoom

fierce (heat)—shadeed

finish—khallaS (II)

fire (n.); open fire—naar (*pl.*
neeraan); fataH an-neeraan

flies (insects)—dabbaan (*sing.*
dabbaana)

float—9aam byi9oom

fly (vb)—Taar, byiTeer,
Tayaraan

for—min shaan, la- (+
pronouns), min 'ajl

foreigner—'ajnabee (*pl.*
ajaanib)

Forget it! (slang)—bi-laa-haa!

fork—shawka (*pl.* shuwak)

free—Hurr (*pl.* 'aHraar)

free (no charge)—bi-laash

free (no work)—faaDee (*pl.*
-een)

French—faransaawee (*pl.* -een)

friend—Sadee' (*pl.* 'aSdi'aa)

friend, owner—SaaHib (*pl.*
'aSHaab)

from—min

G

gate, door—baab (*pl.* 'abwaab)

generous, noble—kareem (*pl.*
kiraam)

get acquainted with—ta9arraf
(V) 9ala

girl, daughter—bint (*pl.*
banaat)

give and take (n.)—'akhd oo
radd

glad: be glad—fariH, byifraH,
faraH

go—raaH, byirooH

go down—nazal, byinzal,
nuzool

go in—dakhal, byudkhul,
dukhool

go out—kharaj, byukhruj, khurooj

go out of one's mind—Taar 9a'lo

go up—Tala9, byiTla9, Tuloo9

God—allaah (jalla jalaaluhu, 9azza wa jall, subHaan wa ta9aala, *etc.*; *see Lesson seventeen*)

good—Hasan, Tayyib, kuwayyis, 9aal

Good Friday—al-jum9a al-9aZeema

goodbye—bi-khaaTrak (*by person leaving*), ma9 as-salaama (*by one remaining*)

good-for-nothing—mush naafi9

grain (wheat)—Habba (*pl.* Habbaat)

grandfather—jidd (*pl.* 'ajdaad, 'ujdood)

great, big—kabeer (*pl.* Kibaar), 9aZeem

green—'akhDar

greet—sallam (II) 9ala

greeting—salaam, taHeea (*pl.* -aat, *for both*)

ground—'arD

grounds: on the grounds that . . . —9ala 'asaas 'inno . . .

group—jamaa9a (*pl.* -aat)

grow (cultivate)—zara9, byizra9, ziraa9a

grow old—shaab, byisheeb, shayb

guide (n.)—daleel

guide (vb)—dall, byidill, dallaala

H

had: You had better go— 'aHsan tarooH

haggle—shaaraT (III)

hair—sha9r (*pl.* -aat)

hand—yad *or* eed (*pl.* aydee, *or* dayyaat *in some dialects*)

hand in hand—fee eed ba9D

hang, suspend—9alla' (II)

happen; It happened that . . . —Hadas, byuHdus, Hudoos; saa'abat inno . . .

happy—sa9eed (*pl.* su9adaa), farHaan (*pl.* -een)

have—(*see Lesson two ff.*)

he—huwa

head—raas (*pl.* ru'oos)

head over heels—ra'san 9ala 9aqab

hear—sami9, byisma9, sam9

heart—'alb (*pl.* 'uloob)

help—saa9ad (III)

here—hawn

here is—hayy (+ *pronouns*)

hexagon—musaddas

hit—Darab, byuDrub, Darb

honeymoon—shahr il-9asal

honour (n.)—sharaf, 9ard/9irD (*see Lesson eighteen*)

honour (vb)—karram (II), sharraf (II)

hospital—mustashfa (*pl.* mustashfayaat)

hot—Haar, Haamee, sukhn

hotel—fundu' (*pl.* fanaadi')

hour—saa9a (*pl.* -aat)

house—bayt (*pl.* buyoot)

How?—kayf?

How much/many?—kam?
'addaysh?
Hullo!—marHaba!
humour (vb)—saayar (III)
hurry: in a hurry, 'express'—
musta9jal

I

idea—fikra (*pl.* fikar, 'afkaar)
idiot—ghabee (*pl.* 'aghbeeaa)
if—(*see Lesson eleven*)
imagine—taSawwar (V)
impossible—mustaHeel
in—fee
in: He's not in—mush mawjood
in order to/that—min shaan
incapable of—9aajiz 9an
influence—nufooz; waasTa (*see
Lesson eighteen*)
information—ma9loomaat
inside—juwwa; daakhil
inside out—bil-ma'loob
insist on—'aSarr (IV) 9ala
intense—shadeed
interested: be interested in—
ihtamm (VIII) fee
interesting—(*see Lesson
seventeen*) mufeed *etc.*
introduce (someone) to; get to
know—9arraf (II) (someone)
9ala; ta9arraf 9ala
invite—9azam, byi9zam, 9azm;
da9a, byid9ee, da9wa

J

jar—jarra (*pl.* -aat)
joking: I'm not joking—mush
9am bamzaH

Jordan—'al-'urdun
Jordanian—'urdunee (*pl.* -een)
journalism—SaHaafa
journalist—SuHufee (*pl.* -een)
joy, wedding celebration—
faraH (*pl.* 'afraaH)
judge—'aaDee (*pl.* 'uDaa(t))
just: He's just come—ba9do
jaaee
Just so!—biZ-Zabt!

K

kidding: No kidding!—laa!
SaHeeH!
kindly: Would you
kindly . . . ?—luTfan
knife—sikkeen(a) (*usually f.*;
pl. sakaakeen)
know; as far as I know—9araf,
byi9raf, ma9rifa; 9ala 9ilmee
knowledge, science—9ilm (*pl.*
9uloom)
kohl—kuHl
Koran—al-qur'aan al-kareem
etc. (*see Lesson seventeen*)

L

labour, hard—'a9maal shaa''a
lack (n.)—9adam
lack (vb): He lacks nothing—
maa byun'uSo shee
lamp—faanoos (*pl.* fawaanees)
land: by land—barran
language—lugha (*pl.* -aat)
last: At last! the last one; last
year—(wa) akheeran! aakhir
waaHid; is-sana il-maaDya

late: the late Mr X—
il-marHoom

laugh (at)—DaHak, byiDHak,
DaHk (9ala)

lead (vb)—'aad, byi'ood,
'eeaada

learn—ta9allam (V)

learned: a learned man—
9allaama, muta9allim

leave, abandon—tarak,
byutruk, tark

Lebanese—lubnaanee (pl.
-een)

Lebanon—lubnaan

let (Let's go!), leave—khalla
(II)

letter—maktoob (pl.
makaateeb)

lies: pack of lies—kizb fee kizb

life—Hayaa(t)

like (prep.)—mitl

like, love—Habb, byiHibb,
Hubb

line, track, route—khaTT (pl.
khuTooT)

little: a little—shwayy, 'aleel

live, dwell—sakan, byuskun,
sakan

long for, miss—'ishtaa' (VIII)

lost: get lost—Daa9, byiDee9,
Deeaa9

lunch (n.); have lunch—ghada;
taghadda (V)

M

make, do—9amil, bya9mal,
9aml

man—rajul (pl. rijaal)

mankind—al-insaan

map—khaarTa (pl.
kharaayiT)

market—soo' (pl. 'aswaa')

mason—Hajjaar (pl. -een)

mass (in church)—'uddaas (pl.
'adaadees)

may (possibly)—mumkin
(followed by non-past vb)

means: by no means—laa,
abadan!

meet—laa'a (III)

meet each other—'ilta'a (VIII),
byilta'ee ta'aabal (VI), talaa'a
(VI)

mercy: have mercy on—raHim,
byirHam, raHma

middle—wasaT

middle aged—fee mutawassiT
al-9umr

mile—meel (pl. 'amyaal)

mind (intellect); easy in mind;
set his mind on; went out of
his mind—9a'l (pl. 9u'ool);
murtaaH il-baal; HaaTit
bi-fikro; Taar 9a'lo

minute (n.)—da'ee'a (pl.
da'aayi')

Miss—al-aanisa

mistake—ghalTa or ghalaT (pl.
ghalTaat)

money—fuloos, maSaaree,
miSriyyaat, maal

money-changer—Sarraaf (pl.
-een)

month—shahr (pl. shuhoor)

months of the year—(see
Lesson seventeen)

morning—SabaaH

morning: in the morning—
SabaaHan

moron—tees (*pl*. tuyoos)

Moslem, Muslim—muslim (*pl*.
muslimeen)

much—kateer, 'ikteer

must—laazim, Darooree (*see
Lesson four*)

my dear—Habeebee

N

nation—'umma (*pl*. umam)

national—waTanee

natural, patriotic—Tabee9ee

naturally, of course—
Tab9an

nature—Tabee9a

necessary—Darooree, laazim

neck: He got it in the neck—
Hara'oo lo deeno/bayto

neighbour—jaar (*pl*. jeeraan)

never mind—maa 9alaysh

new—jadeed (*pl*. judud),
'ijdeed (*pl*. 'ijdaad)

newspaper—jareeda (*pl*.
jaraayid)

New Year's Day—9eed ra's is-
sana

next to—bi-jaanib, Hadd

nine-fold—tusaa9ee

no—laa

noon—Duhr/Zuhr

north—shimaal

not—mush, laa/maa

not yet—mush . . . ba9d, lissa
(li-has-saa9a)

now; from now on—halla, issa;
min halla oo Taali9

number—numra

numbers—(*see Lesson two,
Appendix*; *for adjectives see
Lesson five*)

O

obliged: much obliged—
mamnoon (+ *pronouns*)

octet—tumaanee

odd (number)—fardee

offer (to)—9araD, byi9raD,
9arD (9ala)

office—maktab (*pl*. makaatib)

officer—DaabiT (*pl*.
DubbaaT), ZaabiT (*pl*.
ZubbaaT)

official—rasmee

official, employee—muwaZZaf
(*pl*. -een)

OK, fine—Tayyib

on—9ala

one: Anyone there?—fee
Had(a) hunaak?

one-eyed—'a9war

only, but—bass

open; opened—fatah; maftooH

opened; be opened—'infataH

open-minded—munfatiH

opinion—ra'ee (*pl*. 'aaraa')

opportunity, chance—furSa (*pl*.
furaS)

oppose—9aaraD (III)

or—'aw

order: out of order; in order
to—mu9aTTal, kharbaan,
9aTlaan; Hatta

other—taanee, 'aakhar, ghayr

outside—barra

outstanding, excellent—
mumtaaz

overdid: they overdid things—
takhkhanoo-haa

owe: I owe you a lira—9alay-lak
leera

owner—SaaHib (*pl.* 'aSHaab)

P

pain (n.)—'alam (*pl.* 'aalaam)

pain (vb)—waja9, byooja9,
waj9

pair—zawj/jawz (*pl.* 'azwaaj)

Palestine—filisTeen

Palestinian—filisTeenee (*pl.*
-een)

pardon: I beg your pardon; I
beg pardon of God!—
9afwan; 'astaghfir 'allaah!

park (vb)—wa' 'af (II)

particular (e.g. reason)—
mu9ayyan

pass, elapse—faat, byifoot,
fawaat

past (n.)—maaDee

pay (vb)—dafa9, byidfa9, daf9

peace—salaam, silm, SulH

peaceful (e.g solution)—silmee

peasant—fallaaH (*pl.* -een)

people (in general)—naas

people (e.g. the French)—
sha9b (*pl.* shu9oob)

photograph (vb)—Sawwar (II)

pilgrimage—Hajj

Pillars of Islam—'arkaan
al-islaam

pimp (professional!)—gawwaad
(*pl.* -een), 9ars, 9akroot

pity: What a pity!—yaa
Haraam! yaa khasaara!

place—maHall (*pl.* -aat),
makaan (*pl.* amaakin)

please: Yes please—min faDlak

pleased: be pleased with—
raDee 9an

poet—shaa9ir (*pl.* shu9araa)

poetry—shi9r

praise (n.)—Hamd

prayer—Salaa(t) (*pl.* Salawaat)

precede, get ahead of—saba',
byusbu', saba'

prefer . . . to . . .—faDDal
(II) . . . 9ala . . .

prepare, make ready—HaDDar
(II)

present (intransitive); be
present—ista9add (X);
HaDar, byuHDur, HuDoor

present, 'there'—mawjood

priest—khooree (*pl.*
khawaarina)

prince—'ameer (*pl.* 'umaraa)

private—khaaS, khuSooSee

proceed, march—saar, byiseer,
sayr

producer (e.g. film)—mukhrij
(*pl.* -een)

professor—'ustaaz (*pl.*
'asaatiza)

programme—barnaamaj (*pl.*
baraamij)

progress (vb)—ta'addam (V)

prophet—rasool (*pl.* rusul)

pronounce—lafaZ, byulfuZ,
lafZ

prostitute—sharmooTa (*pl.*
sharaameeT)

punish—'aaSaS (III)
put—HaTT, byiHuTT, HaTT
put on (clothes)—labis, byilbas,
libaas

Q

quadrilateral, quatrain—
rubaa9ee
queer (sex)—shaaz
question; It's a question
of . . .—su'aal (pl. 'as9ila),
mas'ala (pl. masaa'il);
il-mas'ala mas'alat . . .
quick-witted—saree9 il-khaaTir
quiet: keep quiet!—'uskut!
quintet—khumaasee

R

rain (n.)—shitaa
rain (vb)—shattat (II)
(id-dunya)
rather: or rather—'aw bil-aHra
read—'araa, byi'raa, 'iraaya
ready—Haadir, musta9idd,
jaahiz
really, truly—Ha'ee'a
reason; by reason of—sabab
(pl. 'asbaab); bi-Hukm
receive (guests)—ista'bal (X)
red: be red, become red—
'aHmar, iHmarr
regain—istarja9 (X)
relate, tell (story), speak—
Haka, byiHkee, Hikaaya
relation: in relation to (as for)—
bin-nisba 'ila
relations—'araayib

relax, rest—istaraaH (X)
religion—deen (pl. 'adyaan)
rely on—ittakal 9ala (VIII)
remain—Zall/Dall, byiDall,
Dall; ba'ee, byib'aa, ba'aa
renew—jaddad (II)
repetition—tikraar
residence—manzil (pl.
manaazil)
respect—iHtaram (VIII)
respond to—istajaab li (X)
return, come back; in return
for—raja9, byirja9, rujoo9;
mu'aabil
revenge—taar
revolver—musaddas (pl. -aat)
right (correct)—SaHeeH
right (and left)—yameen (oo
yasaar/shimaal)
rise, get up—'aam, byi'oom,
'eeaam
room—ghurfa (pl. ghuraf)
Rubbish!—kalaam faaDee!
rule (vb)—Hakam, byuHkum,
Hukm

S

same, self—nafs (e.g. nafs
is-saa9a)
say, tell—'aal, byi'ool, 'awl
saying: as the saying goes—
mitl-maa byi'ooloo
scholar—9aalim (pl. 9ulamaa)
school—madrasa (pl. madaaris)
Search me! (How do I know?!)
—shoo baa9rifnee?
sect—Taa'ifa (pl. Tawaa'if)
see—shaaf, byishoof

send—'arsal (IV)

send back—rajja9 (II)

send down, put down—nazzal, 'anzal

sergeant—shaaweesh (*pl.* shawaaweesh)

settle (land)—istawTan (X) isteeTaan

she—hiya

shepherd—raa9ee (*pl.* ru9aa(t))

shop—dukkaan (*f.*; *pl.* dakaakeen)

sick to death of—zah'aan min

simple, easy—baseeT

simple (-minded), 'nice'—darweesh

since, because—*see Lesson eight*

sincerely; yours sincerely—al-mukhliS

sing—ghanna (II)

Sir (Dear sir)—yaa seedee

sister—'ukht (*pl.* 'akhawaat)

sit—jalas, byijlis, juloos; 'u9ud, byu'9ud, 'u9ood

situated: be situated—byoojad

situation, position—maw'if (*pl.* mawaa'if), waDa9 (*pl.* 'awDaa9)

slave—9abd (*pl.* 9abeed)

sleep—naam, byinaam, nawm

small, young—Sagheer (*pl.* Sighaar)

smoke (vb)—dakhkhan (II)

so big (demonstration)—hal-'add

so-and-so—fulaan

society (e.g. news)—mujtama9 (*pl.* -aat)

son—'ibn (*pl.* 'abnaa)

sound, healthy—saleem, SaHeeH

south—janoob

speak—takallam (V)

speaking: It's . . . speaking—'ana . . .

specialize (in)—takhaSSaS (V) (fee)

spend a summer holiday—Sayyaf (II)

spirit—rooH (*pl.* 'arwaaH)

spite: in spite of—ghaSban 9an

spoon—mal9a'a (*pl.* malaa9i')

spring—rabee9

square—murabba9

stand—wa'af, byoo'af, wu'oof

state (political)—dawla (*pl.* duwal)

steal—sara', byusru', sara'a

stick, crook—9aSa (*pl.* 9aSaaya)

still (e.g. He's still here)—ba9do hawn

stock: of good stock—najeeb

stomach—baTn (*pl.* buToon)

stone—Hajar (*pl.* 'aHjaar)

stop (intransitive)—tawaqqaf (V)

stop (transitive)—wa''af

street—shaari9 (*pl.* shawaari9)

study (vb)—daras, byudrus, diraasa

success—najaaH

successful: be successful—tawaffa'

suggestion—'i'tiraaH (*pl.* -aat)

summer—Sayf

sun—shams

sunset—maghrib

sweet; find sweet—Heloo; 'istaHla (X)

Syria—soorya, ish-shaam

Syrian—sooree, shaamee (*pl.* -een)

T

table; dining table—Taawila (*pl.* -aat); sufra

tail—danab (*pl.* 'adnaab)

take—'akhad, byaakhud, 'akhd

take away—shaal, byisheel

take off (clothes)—shalaH, byishlaH

taste: good taste—zaw' (NB often equivalent to English 'common sense')

teach—9allam (II)

teacher—mu9allim (*pl.* -een)

tear out, uproot—khala9, byikhla9, khal9

telephone—tilfon (*pl.* -aat), haatif (*pl.* hawaatif)

tentmaker—khayyaam (*pl.* -een)

testify—shahad, byish-had, shahaada

testimony, certificate—shahaada (*pl.* -aat)

than—min

thank—shakar, byushkur, shukr

Thanks!—shukran!

that (conjunction)—(*see Lesson eight*)

that (demonstrative)—had(h)aak

that is to say; . . . er . . :—ya9nee

then (i.e. 'and then . . .')—oo ba9dayn

there is/are—fee

therefore, and so—Li-hayk

they—hum

think—'iftakar (VIII)

this—haad(h)a

throw—rama, byirmee, ramee

throw out, expel—'akhraj (IV)

thus so—hayk

ticket—tazkira (*pl.* tazaakir)

to (prep.)—'ila

today—il-yawm

tomorrow—bukra (*often in Lebanon followed by* 9aa bukra)

tongue, language—lisaan (*pl.* 'alsina/'alsun)

tonight—il-layla

too (e.g. 'too big')—kabeer, 'ikbeer

translate—tarjam, byitarjim, tarjama

travel—saafar (III)

tree—shajara (*pl.* shajar/'ashjaar)

triangle—muthallath

tribe—qawm, qabeela, 9asheera, jamaa9a

trilateral—thulaathee

trip, visit—mishwaar (*pl.* mashaaweer)

true, correct—SaHeeH

try—jarrab (II)

U

ugly—'abeeH, 'ibaaH

uncle—9amm, khaal

under—taHt, 'a'all min ('*less than*')

understand—fahim, byifham, fahm

unfortunate—miskeen (*pl.* masaakeen)

unique—fareed

united: be united—ittaHad, yattaHid, ittiHaad

unlucky (jinxed)—manHoos

up to (now)—li-ghaayat . . .

upright, honest—SaaliH (*pl.* -een)

use (vb)—istakhdam (X)

use: It's no use—maa fee(sh) faayida

utmost: do one's utmost—9amil il-mustaHeel

V

valley—waadee (*pl.* widyaan)

very—'ikteer (*following the adj.*)

view: in view of the circumstances—naZaran li- . . .

village—qarya (*pl.* quraa), Day9a (*pl.* Dee9)

Virgin, the—9adraa

virtue: by virtue of—bi-faDl

visit—zaar, byizoor, zeeaara

W

wait—intaZar (VIII), istanna (*conjugates like Form I doubled vb*)

wake up (intransitive)—istay'aZ (X)

wake up (transitive)—wa99a (II)

walk—masha, byimshee, mashee

want to: I want to—biddee (*followed by a non-past vb*)

wash (vb)—ghassal (II)

water—mayy (*pl.* -aat)

watermelon—baTTeekh (*pl.* baTTaayikh)

waterspout—mizraab (*pl.* mazaareeb)

we—'iHna, naHn, niHna

wear (vb)—labis, byilbas, libaas

wedding—(Haflat) 9urs/zafaaf, faraH

week—'usboo9 (*pl.* 'asaabee9)

weep, cry—baka, byibkee, bakaa

weight: net weight—wazn Saafee

welcome (vb)—raHHab (II) bi

well, fit, happy—mabsooT

west—gharb

What?—shoo?

whatever (etc.)—(*see Lesson ten*)

When?—'aymta?

Where?—wayn? fayn?

Which?—ayy?

which (relative pronoun)—'illee

while—baynamaa

Whit Sunday—9eed il-9anSara

white—'abyaD

Who?—meen?

whole, complete—kaamil

Why?—laysh? lay?

will (future tense)—raaH
(indeclinable: *followed by vb in non-past*)

wine—nabeed

winter—shitaa

wise—Hakeem (*also = 'doctor'*)

with—ma9

without—bidoon, bilaa

woman—mara (*pl.* niswaan)

wonder: I wonder . . .—yaa
turaa . . .

wood—khashab (*pl.* -aat)

word—kalima (*pl.* -aat)

work—'ishtaghal, byishtaghil

world—9aalam

write—katab, byuktub, kitaaba

write to one another—takaatab

writer—kaatib (*pl.* kuttaab)

written: be written—'inkatab

Y

year—sana (*pl.* sineen,
sanawaat); Happy New Year!
—kull sana/9aam oo int bi-
khayr!

yes—na9am, aywa, 'ayy na9am!

yet: not yet—lissa, mush . . .
ba9d

you—inta

youths—shabaab

Z

zero—Sifr

BIBLIOGRAPHY

Cowell, M. W., *Reference Grammar of Syrian Arabic*, Georgetown, 1964.

Driver, G. R., *A Grammar of the Colloquial Arabic of Syria and Palestine*, London, 1925.

Farha, H. T., *Courtesy Expressions in Spoken Arabic*, Beirut, 1971.

Middle East Centre for Arab Studies (MECAS), 'The spoken Arabic of the Levant', unpublished, Shemlan, Lebanon, 1958.

Nasr, R. T., *An English Colloquial Arabic Dictionary*, Beirut, 1972.

Rice, F. and Said, M., *Eastern Arabic*, Beirut, 1960.

Stowasser, K., *Dictionary of Syrian Arabic*, Georgetown, 1964.